Becoming a
GRACIOUS
WOMAN

Becoming a
GRACIOUS
WOMAN

Living a Life of Order,
Kindness and Beauty

Shelly Chen

To: Douglas and my three sons, who have each made me a better woman.

Preface

I have always been inspired by portraits and stories of women from the past. I imagine gracious women sipping tea on a wisteria strewn porch, discussing the virtues of family and home while the children play quietly in the garden, a garden that looks like something out of a Thomas Kinkade painting. Fast forward to my life today and there are days when I find myself struggling just to find a moment's quiet to return a phone call or catch up on weekly tasks. Between taking my children hither and yonder, checking email and trying to stay on top of the ever-growing mountain of household chores, I often wonder where we have gone wrong.

The truth is that as I think about how to live a gracious life, I find myself falling short in every respect. I aspire to be a gracious wife and mother, and yet I know that I fail in so many ways, every day. It is a journey with stops and starts. And so, it is with an honest heart that I write this book. I don't write from the perspective of one who has mastered it, but as one who continues to look towards the goal of becoming the gracious woman I know I was created to be. I hope you will join me along the journey.

Table of Contents

Chapter One

GRACIOUS LIVING:
A Primer

"A gracious woman attains honor…"
(Proverbs 11:16)

THE GRACIOUS WOMAN

Godly. Elegant. Beautiful. These are some words that come to mind when I imagine what a gracious woman is like. She is kind, generous, and open. She radiates warmth, acceptance and joy. She lives her life with purpose, confidence and dignity. The gracious woman has a sense of calling in her life. She has an authentic love for God and an unhurried appreciation of others. Her life is full of purpose and she creates beauty around her. She is more than just charming; she is genuine in her character and sincere in her interest in others.

The novelist Alex Waugh described being in the presence of a gracious woman as "being drawn into a circle where everything is fresher, cleaner; where there is peace, warmth, comfort…. The gracious woman puts a man on trial in the sense that she produces in him the desire to be his best."[1] Indeed, a gracious woman elevates the atmosphere everywhere she goes and all those around her can sense her warm, radiant spirit.

From the time we were little girls, we as women have longed to become gracious women. We set up tea parties and play dress up with Mom's hats and jewelry. Here we mimic the finest qualities of womanhood. But somewhere along the way, the busyness of life and the pressures of other things crowd in and we find ourselves frequently taxed and often ungracious. We snap at our children, grumble at our husbands and find keeping home a burden. But God gave women a special capacity to reflect his grace. We are called to be gracious in every sphere we move it, whether at home or at church or in the community. By God's grace, we can be a reflection of his character and a blessing to others.

But what exactly does it mean to be a gracious woman? The words bring to mind fashionable ladies sipping tea on their front porches. We think of glossy magazines with pictures of lush floral arrangements and beautiful houses. Maybe it is the ability to host a social gathering with artful food and lively conversation. We think being gracious must have something to do with manners, with saying the right things or even wearing the right clothes. But that is not what being a gracious woman is truly all about.

Living graciously begins by understanding what is God's calling for us as Christian women. Our lives and everything we do can have purpose and meaning as we place God in the proper place in our hearts, as King and Lord, and allow His order and design to mold our hearts. Our lives are not meant to be lived aimlessly, but with direction. And God has a plan for every area of our lives, from how we love our husbands to how we raise our children or how we perform at our jobs. As we begin to recognize and understand the significance of what we do as women, even the everyday tasks that we put our hands to can become infused with new meaning and purpose. Knowing God's calling for our lives brings direction and significance to everything we do.

When we understand God's purpose for our lives, we will naturally begin to live a more gracious life. God is all about grace and we as Christian women, will reflect His grace in our desires, words and actions. Although there are many facets to being a gracious woman, we will focus on three guiding principles: **order**, **kindness** and **beauty**.

To live our lives with *order* means that everything is put in the right place. Psalm 50:23b tells us that "to him who orders his way aright, I shall show the salvation of God." God wants us to live an orderly life, not a chaotic one. We must have a respect for the way things should be, and the personal discipline needed to live an ordered life. But order isn't just following a list of rules, but must originate in the heart. So much of our actions and responses to life flow out of our emotions and affections, and God wants them to be made right through our relationship with Him. When we keep God as Lord of our hearts, then our other relationships fall in their rightful place, in order behind him. Living an ordered life also affects our daily routines and personal habits. Order can be far-reaching. It can change how we prioritize our schedules and organize our homes. God wants us to live disciplined, orderly lives. By doing so, we will reflect the rightness of His design in our lives

Secondly, being a gracious woman is being a *kind* woman. Colossians 3:12 says, "Therefore, as God's chosen people, holy and dearly loved, clothe yourselves with compassion, kindness, humility, gentleness and patience." We are to be *covered* in kindness! Our world is a harsh one. Most people don't have time for a kind word, much less for a civil one at times. Gracious living is more than having good manners and knowing the proper way to behave. To be truly gracious is to have a genuine concern for other people, to be able to look outside the sometimes rigid spheres of our own lives and enter into the world of others. To be kind is to have a soft and gentle heart that is open to other people, especially to others that are outside of our normal circle of friends. When we truly make it a point to be kind to others we find that we have to slow down the pace of our lives in order to make room for people. Hurry is a hindrance to kindness, and so becoming gracious involves slowing down enough to love people. Gracious living is marked by kindness.

Finally, gracious living brings true **beauty** into our lives and the lives of those around us. As Christians, we sometimes think of beauty in merely external terms, as something superficial with which truly "spiritual" women will not be preoccupied. We think of beauty only in terms of clothes and home furnishings. But God created true beauty, and He wants us to appreciate and cultivate it. 1 Peter 3:4 tells us that as Christian women, we are to have "unfading beauty" that is "of great worth in God's sight." True beauty is a reflection of goodness and the joy of living that God wants us all to experience.

God created beauty and we were created to respond instinctively to it. Don't our hearts burst at the beauty of God's creation in nature? We look at a sunset or a field of wildflowers and are awed by beauty. We look at our baby's first smile and we are convinced that there is nothing more beautiful. We were created to recognize and respond to true beauty because it is a reflection of God's goodness and love for us. And as our hearts are filled with God's grace, our lives will produce beauty all around us. A heart full of love produces a life full of beauty.

Now that we have some idea what gracious living is all about, how do we know that gracious living is something we are meant to experience today, in our real day to day lives? After all, many of us are struggling with getting our own lives together and keeping our heads barely above water. Are we really equipped to become gracious women? Let's begin by looking at how we as women were created and how we were designed for gracious living.

CREATED BY DESIGN

The pages of the Bible begin with the curious story of God creating the heavens and the earth. Light is separated from darkness and water is divided from the land. The sun, moon, and stars appear on the vast canvas of the universe while a multitude of birds fill the sky and fish swarm the seas.

In this display of God's awesome power, the narrative suddenly focuses in on a little Garden where a man is deciding what to name the animals. When he has finally finished seeing all the animals in creation, the man realizes that none among them is quite like him. God causes the man to fall asleep and then He mysteriously removes one of his ribs. While the man is sleeping, God creates a woman from the rib. The Hebrew word used in this passage expresses the idea of someone carefully building and sculpting a work of art. Think of a master artist meticulously carving a piece of stone, transforming it into a magnificent reflection of beauty. What attention to detail and design he puts into his work! Did you know that, as a woman, you are God's masterpiece? You were created by His design? He designed your entire being to reflect His beauty and character.

God designed women to be uniquely different from men. In fact, the Bible uses two different words to describe how He created men and women. When God made Adam, the word used suggests someone roughly kneading clay. When God created Eve, the word used conveys the idea of a sculptor meticulously chiseling out a work of art. Contrast that to the work of a sculptor meticulously chiseling out his work of art. That is not to say that either sex is better than the other, but the truth is that men and women are different. Even our physical appearance betrays this truth. A woman's body is not the same as a man's body. The proportion of a man's bones and muscles are the same as a woman's. A woman's body is designed softer and gentler, created to bear and nurture life. God created both man and woman, and together masculinity and femininity reflects His nature. As women, we should not be ashamed of our "feminine" traits. They do not make us inferior in any way. Instead, our femininity is a distinguishing crown that uniquely reflects God's glory.

As women, we are called to be women: strong, beautiful, godly women! We are called to reflect the femininity that we were designed for in all its strength and courage, its gentleness and gracefulness. That is the heart of gracious living: to embrace our God-given feminine nature and become all that He calls us to be. Emilie Barnes says it beautifully in her book, *The Spirit of Loveliness.*

> Being a woman created by God is such a privilege - and the gift of our femininity is something we can give both to ourselves and to the people around us. Just one flower, one candle, can warm up a cold, no-nonsense atmosphere with an aura of "I care." Women have always had the ability to transform an environment, to make it comfortable and inviting. I believe we should rejoice in that ability and make the most of it... The spirit of femininity is so many things... It is people accepted and nurtured, loveliness embraced and shared. More important, the spirit of femininity is the spirit of care and compassion. In my mind, the most feminine woman is one with an eye and ear for others, and a heart for God.[2]

Becoming a gracious woman is becoming a true woman, as God designed, one who is filled with God's grace and embraces her femininity with courage and conviction. You were uniquely designed for gracious living!

But can you live a gracious life if you do not know the One Who created you for it? Every woman on earth has been created in God's image to live rightly

> ๛
>
> "THE FACT THAT I AM A WOMAN DOES NOT MAKE ME A DIFFERENT KIND OF CHRISTIAN, BUT THE FACT THAT I AM A CHRISTIAN DOES MAKE ME A DIFFERENT KIND OF WOMAN."
>
> *Elizabeth Elliott*

and to love purely. But the Bible tells us that every one of us has sinned and is incapable of doing the good we want to do through our own strength and efforts. We need to be reconciled to God, and He has provided a way to do so: through Jesus Christ.

We must come to God by acknowledging that we are sinners in His sight and need forgiveness. God so loved us that He gave His only Son Jesus Christ to die on the cross for us and to bring us into a right relationship with God. Jesus' death and resurrection provided the way for us to be reconciled to God. We must believe in Him and surrender our lives to Him, so that He can be Lord of our hearts. If you have not yet made a decision to give your life to Christ, you can do so today! This is the first step towards becoming the gracious woman you were created to be.

If you have already committed your life to Christ, then you have begun your own wonderful journey of becoming the gracious woman you were created to be. As you continue walking with God each day, He will draw you closer to Himself and you will begin to reflect His image. II Corinthians 3:18 tells us that "we, who with unveiled faces all reflect the Lord's glory, are being transformed into his likeness with ever-increasing glory, which comes from the Lord, who is the Spirit." That is the heart of truly gracious living.

The next chapters will look at a gracious woman, inside and out, and how the three main principles of gracious living are reflected in the three main roles of a woman: as a wife, mother and friend, and in her three main areas of influence: her home, work and works of service. I invite you to join the journey towards becoming a gracious woman. It is an exciting life we were created for!

REFLECT AND RESPOND

1.   What comes to mind when you think of
       "Gracious Living"?

2.   Name one area of your life which you feel
       could use more order.

3.   How would you define *kindness*? What is the
       opposite of kindness?

4.   God created a beautiful world. How does
       appreciating God's beauty impact your
       everyday life?

5.   Memorize Proverbs 11:16: "A gracious woman
       attains honor..." (NASV).

THE GRACIOUS WOMAN: INSIDE AND OUT

Chapter Two

A GRACIOUS SPIRIT:
A Woman After God's Heart

"A woman who fears the Lord is to be praised..."
(Proverbs 31:30)

THE INVITATION

Inside every truly gracious woman is a gracious spirit. We are called to be women who fear the Lord and women who seek after God's heart. Taking a look at our spiritual lives, the internal workings of our soul, is where we begin our journey to becoming gracious women.

When we receive salvation and enter into a relationship with God, He calls us to live lives that are dramatically greater than anything we could have imagined. God calls us not only to be Christians in name, but vibrant, whole-hearted followers of Christ whose lives have been transformed by His life in us. He invites us to enter into the greatest relationship we can have. The God of the universe loves us so much that He invites us into a love relationship with Him. That is the heart of what it means to be a Christian and the beginning of living a gracious life, to know the God of grace!

The Bible uses the analogy of marriage to describe what our relationship with God should be like. Ephesians 5:22-33 tells us that it is a great mystery, but the relationship between a husband and wife is like the relationship that Christ has with the church, His Bride. Marriage is the most intimate relationship on earth, and one which should be based on love and truth. There is no room for pretense in marriage. But sometimes we see our spiritual lives as less than intimate. Instead, it is sort of like we are dating. We aren't fully committed, and we are more concerned with making a good impression or saying the right things. We view our Christian life in terms of rules we need to follow or doctrines we need to memorize. We mistakenly believe that being a godly woman means doing all the "right" things. Or maybe it is having an extensive knowledge of the Bible and a correct understanding of theology. Sometimes we feel social pressures to modify our behavior so we conform to other women in the church. Whether it is the amount of makeup we wear or which toys we allow our children to play with, we believe that our outward behavior is what really matters. But the truth is that God knows how our lives are really lived each day, and is interested in what is truly going on inside of us. Like a husband, God ultimately wants our hearts. He loves us unconditionally, and when we truly experience His grace, our hearts will respond back in love. When that happens, then what we think and how we act will also start to change. It will be a transformation that begins from the inside out, and not the other way around.

God is interested in who we really are because He loves the *real* person inside, the authentic woman

– wrinkles, warts and all! Who are you, really? What are you thinking about when you lie awake at night, when there is nothing but the sound of your own breathing? Sometimes our days are so filled with activity, chatter, noise, and busyness that we overlook ourselves in all of the commotion. When you are alone and everything is finally quiet, what thoughts run through your head? Are you worried or fearful about the future? Are you anxious about living up to someone else's expectations? Are you living in guilt or shame over something that happened in your past? Regardless of what condition your heart is in at the moment, God wants to meet you there and He invites you to take a deep breath and trust Him. He invites you to take a step closer to Him and let His love embrace you.

ORDERING OUR WAY TO SEEK GOD

We are to be women who are devoted to the Lord. But devotion and passion for God is not something that we can work up or generate through our own efforts. Like most everything truly good in life, even devotion itself is a gift of grace. It is not something we earn or work ourselves up for. We all start out cold in heart and spiritually lukewarm. Only God's Holy Spirit can stir passion and devotion in our hearts. Salvation is God's promise to take our hearts of stone and give us new hearts, living hearts. Ezekiel 11:19 says, "I will give them an undivided heart and put a new spirit in them; I will remove from them their heart of stone and give them a heart of flesh."

While we cannot produce devotion in our lives, we can ask God for it and order our lives in such a way that we are receptive to His grace. We can come before God, just as we are, and tell Him that although we *want* to love Him passionately, our hearts are cold. And He will begin to pour out His love into our hearts. And the funny thing is that God doesn't just infuse us with new energy to love Him and do good works. Instead, He just seems to love us unconditionally. God enjoys us and doesn't make a long list of requirements for us to meet before He will bless us. When we begin to understand how much He loves us, then we will love Him more.

Many married couples make a point of setting aside regular "date night." When I was growing up, my parents had a weekly date. Even if it was just going for a drive to the local ice cream shop and sharing a bowl of ice cream for twenty minutes, they made a point to spend some time alone, just the two of them, and reconnect with each other. Now that I am married, I understand the importance of what they did. Even though husbands and wives see each other every day and spend hours together under the same roof, they often do without really connecting with each other. Sometimes my husband and I get so busy I feel like we are two ships passing in the night. Just as married couples need to plan for one-on-one time, we need to order our lives to include a devotional time with the Lord each day. We can certainly pray throughout the day, driving in the car or heading out the door, but we also need to set aside time to truly concentrate on reconnecting our souls to God.

St. Benedict, in his famous Rule, presented a daily schedule for the rhythm of prayer, praise and reflection. He based his schedule on Psalm 119:164,

"Seven times a day I praise You for Your righteous laws." And so, the monks under his Rule were to rise seven times throughout each day in order to pray, meditate on Scripture and reflect on God's goodness. While I'm not suggesting we adhere to Benedict's schedule, it serves as an example of how we can structure our lives to connect with God each day.

Firstly, set a time and a place where you will have your devotions each day. This will help you get into a regular routine of daily devotions. Every woman is different and has various schedule considerations, but I have found that it is best for me to rise early in the morning, before the rush of the day begins and meet with God as the sun rises. Make sure you set your clock ahead in order to accommodate for your devotions. Keep your Bible, journal and a pen in the same place. You can put everything together in a pretty basket near your favorite chair.

Then, have a structure for your devotions. The first part of a devotional life is reading the Bible. God speaks to us primarily through His Word, the Bible. But there are many ways to read the Bible.

Sometimes we read it for academic purposes, to understand the history of God's dealings with His people. Sometimes we read it to teach others. We read Scripture to prepare for a Bible study or Sunday school class. Devotional Bible reading is reading the Bible with a heart to connect with God. It isn't merely reading through the Bible in order to finish passages and keep up with a schedule, but to really hear what God might be saying to us through His Word. I have found that devotional Bible reading is the most difficult sort of reading to do. It is much easier to plow through chapters of the Bible and gain some understanding of content, but have my heart relatively unchanged. Devotional Bible reading connects the words to the heart.

When you read your Bible in a devotional manner, read each passage slowly and ask God to open your heart. Keep a journal nearby so you can jot down any thoughts you have on the passage. Ask yourself how the passage applies to your own life. If a verse stands out to you, try to commit it to memory and remember it throughout the day.

Devotional Bible reading isn't haphazard though. I am not suggesting you drop your Bible on the table each day and start reading where the pages fall open. Follow a Bible reading plan. Keep bookmarks in your Bible so you recall where you left off. I have done different things over the years, but one of my favorite reading plans had me reading through one passage from each other major portions of the Bible: the Pentateuch, the Wisdom books, the Prophets, the Gospels and the Epistles. I had at least five bookmarks popping out of my Bible at once! It was a good way to connect with each of the major sections in the Bible.

The other main aspect of a devotional life is prayer. Prayer is how we communicate with God. I have also found that I need to have a sense of order in my prayer life or else I easily end up praying only about my immediate physical concerns and those needs of my small circle of family and friends. You can use a prayer journal and record prayer requests as well as answers to prayer. You can use the structure of the Lord's Prayer[3] to guide your requests and petitions. Each of the verses of the Lord's Prayer can be used as a guide for your own prayers: hallowing God's name, praying for God's will and His kingdom purposes, making requests for our daily needs, confessing our sins and forgiving others, and asking for deliverance from temptation and evil. You can also use the written prayers of others as a springboard for your own. Christian writers and saints throughout history have left us with wonderful prayers that we can read, recite and make our own.

Your devotional time can also include memorizing Scripture, reading other Christian books and writing down reflections or questions from your reading. However you structure your devotional time doesn't matter as much as the regularity of meeting with God each day. Make a commitment to have a daily time with the Lord, even if is only fifteen minutes, and see how God will use that time throughout the rest of your day.

Exodus 34:29-35 describes Moses' encounters with God. Whenever he spent time in God's presence, Moses came out with his face radiating the glory of God. The people saw that his entire countenance was aglow with light. That is how we are to live each day. Our times with God should affect the way we do the things we have to do each day. His love will spill out to those we meet throughout the day.

MARKED BY KINDNESS

Once when my husband Douglas and I were in the middle of an argument, our emotions were escalating and our words becoming more heated. One of us made the mistake of "bringing God" into the discussion (or using Him to accuse the other person). We started *reminding* each other of how utterly *un*-Christian the other one was being. At one point I blurted out, "Well, until you start reading your Bible every day, you can't tell me how God would want *me* to act!" To which he replied, "Well, you may read your Bible every day, but you sure aren't acting like it makes any difference!" *Ouch.*

While keeping a devotional life is very

important, it is not a badge of spirituality. True spirituality is not measured by how many times we have read through the Bible or how many minutes we spend in prayer every day. It isn't measured by how many church meetings we attend each month. It would be easy if we could rate our own spirituality (as well as judge others around us) by those external terms. But real godliness is seen in the reality of one's life, by one's character and heart. And one's heart is usually revealed in our interactions with other people. The theologian and devotional writer Andrew Murray wrote:

> It is easy to think that we humble ourselves before God, but our humility towards others is the only sufficient proof that our humility before God is real. A lesson of deepest importance is that the only humility that is really ours is not the kind we show to before God in prayer but the kind we carry with us, and carry out, in our ordinary conduct.... The seemingly insignificant acts of daily life are tests of eternity because they prove what spirit possesses us. It is in our most unguarded moments that we truly show who we are and what we are made of. To know a truly humble person you must follow that one in the common course of daily life.... Humility before

God is nothing if it is not proven in humility before others.[4]

True spirituality is marked by kindness, humility and compassion. And we are only as kind and humble as our daily lives prove us to be. Each day, we are met with fresh opportunities to show the nature of our spirituality through interactions with other people, especially those people we may find difficult to love. Are we kind to people who may irritate us? Are we patient with slow people? Jesus used the same principle – how we treat other people is the best measurement for how we love God. In Matthew 25, Jesus tells a parable about Sheep and Goats. In verse 40 He says, "I tell you the truth, whatever you did for one of the least of these brothers of mine, you did for me." This theme is repeated throughout the Bible. Our love for God is shown through loving people. I John 4:19-21 tells us, "We love because he first loved us. If anyone says, 'I love God,' yet hates his brother, he is a liar. For anyone who does not love his brother, whom he has seen, cannot love God, whom he has not seen. And he has given us this command: Whoever loves God must also love his brother."

Kindness should mark our spiritual lives. But what exactly is kindness? Is it simply being nice to others? Is it looking the other way at sin in order to be tolerant of others? It starts by remembering how kind God has been to us. All of us can look back at our own lives and see how merciful God has been to us. I think back to the kind of person I was before God saved me and I am amazed by His kindness towards me. Romans 2:4 tells us that it is God's kindness that has lead us to repentance. "Or do you show contempt for the riches of his kindness, tolerance and patience, not realizing that God's kindness leads you toward repentance?" God's kindness doesn't keep us mired in our own sinfulness, but transforms our hearts in such a way that our actions and lives are changed from darkness to light.

When we realize how kind God has been to us, we are able to show kindness to others. Jesus is the ultimate example of God's kindness. If you read the Gospels, you will see a picture of God of mercy and kindness. Jesus, who was called a "Friend of Sinners" was open, caring and available. His kindness towards prostitutes and tax gatherers transformed their lives. As society's outcasts and hardened sinners experienced God's kindness, their hearts were softened and their lives changed. As we become more like Jesus we will become women who are characterized by kindness towards others.

Back in the 1990's a phrase coined by a woman named Anne Herbert became popular across America. "Practice random acts of kindness and senseless acts of beauty." It started popping up on t-shirts and bumper stickers. The idea was that human beings can spread kindness through random, unexpected actions like paying the toll for the car behind you or filling up a stranger's parking meter. While those are all lovely ideas for showing kindness to others, kindness goes deeper than mere random acts. We are to be both purposeful and consistent in our kindness.

When we recognize the humanity in people, we begin to treat others with dignity. It is easy to view people as mere tools to make our own lives better. That is how we sometimes treat the cashier at the grocery store. She is a machine paid to get my items through the line in the quickest manner possible. We grimace when she seems inefficient. Instead, we should see that the person behind the register is a human being, perhaps someone with pain in her eyes, a person whom God deeply loves and values. Patience, understanding and a kind word can breathe life back into a dying heart, and that is what showing kindness to others is all about.

THE BEAUTY OF THE LORD

The first question in the Westminster Catechism is: "What is the chief and highest end of man?" The response is, "Man's chief end is to glorify God and to enjoy Him forever." As Christians, we often spend a lot of energy on the first half of that statement, on glorifying God. We talk about glorifying God through our actions and words, through worship and fellowship, through witnessing to others and sharing the Gospel. These are all important aspects of the Christian life. But equally important is simply *enjoying* God for Who He is. The first half of that statement involves our "doing." The second half involves our "being." That is where beholding God's beauty comes into focus.

Have you ever thought about how we respond to beauty? We enjoy something beautiful purely for its own intrinsic value, not for what tasks it performs or how useful it is to us. We enjoy a sunset by taking a deep breath and just gazing at the vivid colors. We enjoy a rose by inhaling its fragrance. We are to enjoy God by basking in His presence. And we can experience His presence everywhere and respond in outward praise or quiet adoration.

> ❧❧
>
> "EARTH'S CRAMMED WITH HEAVEN, AND EVER COMMON BUSH AFIRE WITH GOD; BUT ONLY HE WHO SEES TAKES OFF HIS SHOES — THE REST SIT ROUND IT AND PLUCK BLUEBERRIES."
>
> *Elizabeth Barrett Browning*
> *(1806-1861)*
>
> ❧❧

God is beautiful and we are to enjoy and worship Him as we recognize His presence in the world around us. Psalm 27:4 describes a single-hearted devotion to God. The psalmist is content just to behold His beauty. "One thing I ask of the LORD, this is what I seek: that I may dwell in the house of the LORD all the days of my life, to gaze upon the beauty of the LORD and to seek him in his temple." We can see glimpses of God's beauty all around us if our hearts are open to Him.

Sometimes we catch of glimpse of it in the beauty of nature. Have you been on vacation and hiked to a beautiful place that just takes your breath away? Have you ever walked into a church that is decorated for a wedding and your heart is lifted by the beauty you see? These are all ways that we can experience God's beauty. When we do, we can respond by praising Him in our hearts.

We can also experience God's presence in other people. Sometimes the unexpected kindness of a stranger warms our hearts. A firm hug from a loved one reminds us that God loves us. Seeing a child's face light up when he learns something new makes us feel like we are learning it again for the first time too. These are all ways that we can see God's beauty through other people.

The key is that when we experience life's wonders and these precious moments of beauty, we should remember that God is the author of all that is beautiful and good in this world. We turn our hearts towards Him and thank Him in the simple act of prayer or praise. God wants us to experience His presence regularly and talk to Him in our hearts. When we experience beauty, our response should be to talk to the Creator of beauty.

> God is a person, and in the deep of His mighty nature, He thinks, wills, enjoys, feels, loves, desires and suffers as any other person may. In making Himself known to us He stays by the familiar pattern of personality. He communicates with us through the avenues of our minds, our wills and our emotions. The continuous and unembarrassed interchange of love and thought between God and the soul of the redeemed man is the throbbing heart of New Testament religion.[5]

God wants us to *enjoy* Him and to enjoy all the gifts He has for us. He wants us to receive life with open arms and to gaze at His beauty which surrounds us. If we would just open our spiritual eyes to the world around us, we would see His hand everywhere.

The Heart of a Woman

At the heart of a gracious woman is her inner life, her soul, her spiritual nature. As you cultivate your spiritual life by purposefully ordering your ways to let God in, He will transform your heart to be kind towards others. You will be branded with His love and kindness will distinguish your life. And you will experience the joy of connecting with God as you see glimpses of His beauty all around you. This is the heart of what it is to be a gracious woman.

REFLECT AND RESPOND

1. What does it mean to be a woman for fears the Lord? Can you think of examples of women from the Bible or women that you know who have a heart for God?

2. Have you set aside a time each day to spend with God in Bible reading and prayer? If not, plan a time and place for daily devotions.

3. Think of one way you can show kindness to someone this week.

4. How have you seen God's beauty this week?

5. Memorize Proverbs 31:30: "Charm is deceptive, and beauty is fleeting; but a woman who fears the LORD is to be praised.

Chapter Three

A GRACIOUS BEAUTY:
A Woman and Her Image

"The unfading beauty of a gentle and quiet spirit..."
(1 Peter 3:4)

TRUE BEAUTY

There is something inherent in human nature that appreciates beauty. We marvel at a vibrant sunset, we admire the delicate petals of a rose, we enjoy the result of an artist's creative expression. Perhaps this is because true beauty has within itself qualities of goodness and order. God's creation was of such beauty and order that He proclaimed over it, "It is good!" As we become more gracious on the inside, the natural result is that we will become more beautiful on the outside.

True beauty is a good thing, and is based on internal qualities that shine through our faces, our eyes, our smiles, even our whole bodies. As the fruit of God's Spirit is reflected in our lives, we become truly beautiful. My mother has the most beautiful hands I know. It isn't because she gets manicures or has any special regimen to take care of her skin. In fact, as she gets older, they show the signs that her hands have spent years cleaning, washing and doing housework. My mother's hands are beautiful because of the love they show. They are gentle, kind and compassionate, and that's what makes them truly beautiful.

True ugliness works the same way. Being "ugly" is not something that is external but something that comes from the inside of us. As women, we often focus on our "problem" areas: the extra jiggle around our midsection, those increasing wrinkles around our eyes, our unmanageable tresses. We don't realize that the things that *really* detract from our beauty are not physical but spiritual. Just as true beauty is a reflection of inner qualities, ugliness is a reflection of internal failings. When we have anger, bitterness, jealousy or insecurity in our hearts, it won't be long until those traits are manifest in our faces and even in our bodies. Our shoulders will slump and our faces will show signs of the negative emotions that have been ruling our thoughts. And it won't matter how pretty are clothes are our how much make-up we wear. We won't be able to cover up an ugly spirit on the inside.

Audrey Hepburn, one of the most beautiful women to grace the silver screen, loved the poem "Time-Tested Beauty Tips"[6]. It describes the sort of beauty that comes from the inside of a woman.

> For attractive lips, speak words of kindness.
> For lovely eyes, seek out the good in people.
> For a slim figure, share your food with the hungry.
> For beautiful hair, let a child run his or her fingers through it once a day.
> For poise, walk with the knowledge that you never walk alone.
> People, even more than things, have to be restored, renewed, revived, reclaimed and redeemed; never throw out anyone.
> Remember, if you ever need a helping hand, you'll find one at the end of each of your arms.

As you grow older, you will discover that you have two hands, one for helping yourself, the other for helping others.
The beauty of a woman is not in the clothes she wears, the figure that she carries or the way she combs her hair.
The beauty of a woman must be seen from in her eyes, because that is the doorway to her heart, the place where love resides.
The beauty of a woman is not in a facial mole, but the true beauty in a woman is reflected in her soul. It is the caring that she lovingly gives the passion that she shows.
The beauty of a woman grows with the passing years.

The words of this poem ring true. While she wore some of the most fashionable clothes and had the best makeup artists and hairstylists at her disposal, even Audrey Hepburn recognized that true beauty comes from the heart. Beauty does not come from having perfect teeth, but a genuine smile. Truly beautiful women are those whose beauty grows on others. Some women have faces that could grace a magazine cover, but when they open their mouths, they are crass or bitter. Their physical beauty is just a shiny veneer that hides the warts inside. In addition, there are women who may never turn any heads on the street, but when you get to know their kind and gracious personality, they become more and more beautiful. They have the sort of beauty that is expressed in kindness and grace towards others. Over time, they are the ones whose beauty endures.

> "HER BEAUTY IS NOT A MODEL'S BEAUTY. IT'S THE BEAUTY WE SEE IN SOMEONE AT THE SECOND GLANCE. THE WOMAN WHO TURNS YOU AROUND FROM THE INSIDE, AFTER HOURS OR MAYBE DAYS HAVE GONE BY."
>
> *Steve Martin,*
> *Roxanne*

The Bible teaches us about a woman's true beauty. It is of great worth to God and will not fade with the passage of time. I Peter 3:3-6 tell us that this kind of beauty comes from the internal qualities of a woman who trusts God.

> Your beauty should not come from outward adornment, such as braided hair and the wearing of gold jewelry and fine clothes. Instead it should be that of your inner self, the unfading beauty of a gentle and quiet spirit, which is of great worth in God's sight. For this is the way the holy women of the past who put their hope in God used to make themselves beautiful. They were submissive to their own husbands, like Sarah, who obeyed Abraham and called him her master. You are her

daughters if you do what is right and do not give way to fear.

In this passage, Peter is not saying that we are forbidden from braiding our hair or wearing jewelry, but that our beauty does not come from such external aids. Our beauty, and our efforts towards becoming beautiful, should be focused on developing a spirit that is full of gentleness, trust, integrity and courage.

Gentleness is an attitude of the heart. It is a tenderness and openness to God and to others. We should have softness in our personalities. Gentleness looks on others with kindness and compassion, forgiving wrongs and seeing beyond present failings to what God has called others to become.

Trust is shown in our faith toward God even when we don't understand His ways. We believe and hold fast to the knowledge that God is good and has plans to prosper and bless us, not to harm us. Sarah demonstrated her trust in God when she submitted to her husband Abraham.

Integrity is our commitment to do what is right and to obey God even when others are not looking. Integrity involves a conscious decision to let our actions line up with what we say we believe. It is being consistent in our lives as we are in our words.

Finally, **courage** is our stubborn refusal to be dictated by fear. Living life well takes a lot of courage: courage to love, courage to do what is right, courage to stand up for one's beliefs, courage to hope when all hope seems lost.

Just as we make conscious decisions about what we are going to wear each morning, we should be conscious of choosing to clothe ourselves each day with these qualities.

KEEP ORDER FOR YOUR BODY

The first principle of living graciously is to live an ordered life. Order applies not only to our internal, spiritual lives, but also to our external, physical bodies. I Corinthians 6:19 tells us that because we have received Christ into our hearts as Lord, our bodies are "temples of the Holy Spirit". God's Spirit dwells inside of us, and as such, we should treat our bodies with respect. It is important that we take care of our bodies by practicing healthy habits and a having a consistent, orderly lifestyle. We need order our lives to make sure that we eat well, exercise regularly and get adequate rest.

1.   *Eat Well.* Being conscious of what we put into our bodies will have an effect on how our bodies function. Certain foods, high in cholesterol and fat, may taste good, but in the long run will cause our bodies to feel sluggish and tired. Eat a balanced diet full of fresh vegetables and fruits, whole grains and fiber and do your best to avoid processed foods, saturated fats and red meat. One principle to remember about healthy eating is that the less processed something is, the better it is for you. As foods are processed, preservatives and other chemicals are added and in the process, vitamins and nutrients have been drained out of it. And make sure you vary your diet. Eat different kinds of foods. It will ensure you get the nutrients your body needs as well as keep you interested in your diet.

2.   ***Exercise Regularly.*** This is particularly challenging in our sedentary culture, where much of our work and recreation involves sitting in front of some sort of screen, be it computer or television. But you can start by taking baby steps in the right direction. Plan excursions for exercise into your daily routine. Cardiac exercise, exercise which works the heart, is especially important. Take the stairs instead of the elevator. Park your car farther away from the entrance so you can walk longer.

3.   ***Rest Adequately.*** Our bodies were designed to function best with a good night's sleep each evening. Plan your bedtime according to when you have to rise each morning and stick to it. Make sure you account for time to prepare for bed and wind down mentally. This might mean fifteen minutes to wash, change, and read in bed before turning out the lights. In addition to daily rest, we should have a weekly time of rest. Resting at the end of the week is so important that it is one of the Ten Commandments. Exodus 20:8 tells us to "Remember

the Sabbath day by keeping it holy." God gave us a model for working six days of the week and resting on the seventh. Make sure you plan for an extended time of emotional and physical rest at the end of each week. Keep your weekends as restful and unhurried as possible. Rejuvenate your soul with pleasant slow-paced activities instead of rushing about running errands or catching up on chores. I love Alexandra Stoddard's description of her weekly ritual of rest.

> Saturday is the only day of the week I am unhurried and the only day I don't set an alarm. My body clock awakens me naturally and I let the morning unwrap quietly. This block of time is my treat - I've gotten through the week and have no early appointments, no pressures. I read in bed, and eat from a breakfast tray I set up the night before. I write in my journal and I daydream. There is a certain moment, finally, when I feel an urge to get up, and I spring out of bed full of energy in anticipation of our one fully free day a week. Saturday morning in bed is a ritual I look forward to, now that my children are grown. I look forward to it, Monday through Friday, and relish it on Saturday mornings. It's a good idea to build variety into your daily and weekly rhythms- times and days when you deliberately create a change of pace, do something different from

what you do ordinarily. Saturday morning is one of those times for me.[7]

As we order our lives around taking care of our bodies, we will find that we have more energy and more emotional reserve when the unexpected stresses of life arise. Eating right and exercising regularly will help us feel better about ourselves, and being healthy will be reflected in our attitude and physical appearance.

BE KIND TO YOURSELF AND OTHERS

External beauty is a reflection of internal qualities like kindness and acceptance. The way we view ourselves and other people comes across in our facial expressions and the manner in which we carry ourselves. A beautiful woman is one who accepts herself. She stands tall with poise and confidence because she knows who she is in Christ. Ingrid Trobisch in her book *The Confident Woman* wrote, "It's not enough just to know ourselves. We also want to say yes to who we are, and sometimes that takes courage. If we can't accept ourselves, we can't love ourselves. If we can't love ourselves, we won't be able to love others.… When we reject ourselves, we project our attitude of ourselves onto others."[8]

And so, we must be kind to ourselves. By accepting ourselves, I do not mean that we overlook sin or moral deficiencies. Those are things that we must bring to God and allow Him to deal with in our lives. But we must learn to accept the bodies that God has given us and the natural personalities that inhabit them. Sometimes our "inner judge" is harsher to ourselves than we would ever be to anyone else. *You're fat and ugly. You can't do anything right. Why are you so dumb?* We belittle ourselves in ways we would never say out loud to another person.

As we learn to be kind to ourselves, we also become more accepting of other people, warts and all. People who have unreasonable standards for themselves often have unrealistic expectations for others. But if we recognize that we need God's grace every day, we can be kinder to ourselves when we fail and better able to give grace to other people when they disappoint us too. Being kind to ourselves and others frees us to be genuine with people.

> A gracious woman is never petty or petulant-
> rather she is one who is genuinely interested in
> people and activities. Graciousness gives an
> automatic radiance that magnetizes and, to my
> way of thinking, is the true essence of beauty.
> Instead of fading with the passage of time, the
> graciousness of a personality grows with the
> years.[9]

And so, truly beautiful women are those who not only accept themselves but show kindness and grace to others. Their confidence in Christ gives them a humility that esteems others more highly than themselves. They exude a warmth of personality because they care about others sincerely. We probably all know women whose presence warms and lightens a group. We are glad when they enter the room and something inside of us relaxes when they join a conversation. They calm the social environment and offer humor, warmth and sincerity. This sort of impact is never made because of how someone looks on the outside but the character and personality they have on the inside. That is the essence of true beauty.

Be as Beautiful Outside as You are Inside

The way we look on the outside should be a reflection of the true beauty inside. As we have order in our physical bodies and kindness in our souls, we will be truly beautiful from the inside out. Our physical appearance on the outside should begin to match the genuine beauty we have on the inside.

> ❧❧
> "ALWAYS DRESS IN GOOD TASTE, BUT LET YOUR CHILDREN SEE THAT IT EMPLOYS VERY LITTLE OF YOUR TIME, LESS OF YOUR THOUGHTS, AND NONE AT ALL OF YOUR AFFECTIONS."
>
> *Mrs. Child's The Mother's Book (1931)*
> ❧❧

The way we look on the outside should make us feel good about ourselves. This isn't always the case. There are days when I throw on a pair of old jeans and a sweatshirt, and sweep my hair into a messy ponytail. It is never long before I find myself feeling awkward and insecure, not to mention those always seem to be the days that I end up running into some unexpected acquaintance. Being sloppy by nature, I have been a late bloomer when it comes to believing that my external appearance matters. Couple that with the fact that I used to believe it was unspiritual to care about clothes and makeup. But as I have matured as a Christian and as a woman, I have learned that my external appearance not only affects the way I feel about myself on the inside, but also reflects on my internal qualities. Looking tired and frumpy doesn't make me look more spiritual. It just makes me look tired. But if I put myself together before I step out of the house, I feel more confident about meeting the world head-on. And I present myself in a way that is dignified and reflects honorably on myself. In addition, I also realized that my appearance is a reflection on my husband and family. So, slowly I have begun to recognize that a gracious women is as beautiful on the outside as she is on the inside.

So how do I present myself in the best possible way? Joyce Landort in her book *The Fragrance of Beauty* noted twelve points that describe the physical care of a beautiful woman.

She has clean shining hair.
Her make-up is not heavy, but feminine and soft.
A beautiful woman cares for her fingernails and hands.
She has clean and healthy teeth.
She has regular medical checkups.
She uses deodorant and radiates personal cleanliness.
Her fragrance is definite but gentle and sweet.
She exercises regularly and sticks to a diet, avoiding the appearance of gluttony.
Her whole wardrobe fits her budget.
She uses color to the best advantage
Her speech is not boisterous or profane, but kind.
She avoids unladylike postures and moves with grace.[10]

The overarching message is that a woman should be conscientious her body and personal hygiene. Being healthy, clean and well-groomed is the cornerstone of physical beauty.

I have to admit that I enjoy watching a good makeover show. What always amazes me is that the woman before the makeover is the same woman after the makeover. All along, she had the same potential inside of her. But at the end of the makeover, she is so much more beautiful, poised and confident. The key to her transformation is not any extreme physical changes like cosmetic surgery or aggressive dieting, but discovering how to do more with what she already has. She often learns what style of clothing best suits her body type, what sort of haircut best frames her face and how to apply natural-looking makeup that highlights her existing features. By learning about what looks good on her, she is able to present the best version of herself to the world. So often, she never realized how beautiful she could be. She was inherently beautiful but all it took was recognizing how to bring our her full potential. The three main areas that comprise outward beauty are clothing, hair and make-up.

A gracious woman has an elegant wardrobe, one that is tasteful and classic as opposed to trendy and outlandish. When I think of someone who dressed tastefully, I immediately think of Audrey Hepburn whose impeccable sense of style is still in vogue today. Her clothes were simple but elegant, and her hairstyle and makeup never distracted others from her face. It is better to have a small wardrobe with a few classic, well-tailored clothes made of high-quality material than to have a large wardrobe, with hangers full of "fashionable" clothes which you will probably wear less than two times. Classic clothes are usually very simple, often in solid neutral colors instead of bright patterns, with little embellishment. They keep their form over time and make a woman look elegant and beautiful.

The key to selecting a wardrobe is not only finding your personal style but understanding which clothes suit your age, height and body type. When I entered my late 20s, it started to dawn on me that I should probably stop selecting the bulk of my clothes from the Juniors Department. Even though the sizes might still fit, the styles just didn't suit my age. Likewise, being a small 5'4" (with heels), I have come to accept the fact that I really can't pull off certain clothes that look gorgeous on tall women. There are lots of helpful books and guides that go into detail about which clothes best fit different body types. Once you understand your own body type and what clothes flatter and enhance your body, you should dress in such a way that makes you feel good about yourself. Have you ever asked yourself, "What do my clothes say about me?" A woman's external sense of style is often an expression of her unique inner personality. You can look at some women and see that they are bold and adventurous. Others show that they are creative and artistic. Some reflect a sensitive heart that is drawn to the romantic. Whatever your personality, let your clothing be an expression of who you are to the world. They do not define you, but you define them.

A gracious woman also dresses in a way that respects her own body as well as those that see her. She isn't revealing too much. She appears appropriately dressed for whatever venue she may be going to. Different clothes suit different situations. There are clothes that are appropriate for weddings, other clothes that are proper to wear on vacation, and others that are good for going to the grocery store. It is important to know the difference. We sometimes here the word "modesty" and shudder because we

associate it with peasant skirts and buns. But Francis
Benton defined modesty as simple dressing
appropriately.

> Specific rules about modesty change with the
> styles. Our Victorian ancestors, for instance,
> would judge us utterly depraved for wearing
> the modern bathing suit. Real modesty,
> however, is a constant and desirable quality. It
> is based not on fashion, but on
> appropriateness. A woman boarding a subway
> in shorts at the rush hour is immodest not
> because the shorts themselves are indecent, but
> because they are worn in the wrong place at the
> wrong time. A well-mannered and self-
> respecting woman avoids clothes or behavior
> that is inappropriate or conspicuous.[11]

Secondly, your hairstyle is a lot like your
clothes. It makes an impression for you and can
either enhance or detract from your appearance.
Clean, well-groomed hair is a sign of a healthy woman
who is conscientious of how she presents herself to
the world while an unkempt head of hair can make
your look tired and resigned. Like styles of clothes,
some hairstyles better suit certain face shapes and
ages.

Healthy, glowing skin begins from the inside out. Keeping a healthy diet will not only help you maintain a trim figure but aid in having clear skin. Avoid fatty, breakout-inducing foods. Make sure to exercise regularly and get plenty of sleep. If you smoke, take steps to quit. It is not only detrimental to your lungs and body, but to your skin. Long-time smokers tend to have more wrinkled, ashen skin and can look many years older than they really are. Stick to a daily regimen for healthy skin that includes cleansing, toning and moisturizing.

When it comes to make-up, the key is that you should look as natural as possible. A woman should look radiant, not "made up." The sole purpose of make-up is to conceal blemishes and highlight a woman's natural beauty. Foundation conceals acne and diminishes the look of wrinkles while eye makeup and lipstick bring out a woman's attractive features like her expressive eyes and genuine smile. Heavy, overly bright make-up usually detracts from a woman's natural beauty, and can even make a woman look older than she really is.

Finally, when you step out into the world, walk tall. Have you noticed how some women make cheap clothes look expensive while others wear high-priced clothing and you would never guess they paid as much as they did for them? One reason for this is poise. And the great news is that poise doesn't cost any money! It is something that all women can learn to have. So carry yourself with dignity. Practice good posture by standing and sitting tall. Have confidence in the Lord and remember that He has made you beautiful!

> In the privacy of your bedroom, check the details of your appearance and personal grooming. But when you step out, forget all about the way you look and have confidence in your appearance.[12]

We as women were created to be beautiful! By allowing the Lord to develop His character in our hearts and becoming who He calls us to be, any woman can become truly beautiful from the inside out.

ENDURING BEAUTY

There was an old television series called "The

Golden Girls" which told the story of four single women who shared a house in Miami. They were all in their mid-fifties and older, but were young at heart. In one episode, Rose is having a talk with her boyfriend Miles. She is discouraged and embarrassed as she compares her aging beauty to that of younger women. Miles responds by saying, "When you're young and beautiful, it's an accident of nature. But when you're beautiful older, you've earned it. That you created yourself."[13] There is something to be said about the sort of beauty that is one is not born with, but that one grows into.

True beauty comes from the Lord and will last and even increase over the course of a woman's life. Isn't that a wonderful thing to realize? No wrinkle-reducing cream can promise beauty that actually grows as a woman ages. As we become gracious women, inside and out, our beauty will be one that endures.

REFLECT AND RESPOND

1.   Read I Peter 3:3-6. What do you think this passage is saying about how a woman becomes beautiful?

2.   What practical steps can you take to live a healthier lifestyle? How can you ensure that you eat a balanced diet, make time for exercise and get enough rest?

3.   What kind of attitude do you have towards yourself and other people? Do you find yourself battling your own negative "self talk?" Endeavor to become more positive.

4.   Stand in front of a full-length mirror and look at yourself. How does your reflection make you feel about yourself? Does your appearance reflect your full potential?

5.   Memorize I Peter 3:4: "Instead, it should be that of your inner self, the unfading beauty of a gentle and quiet spirit, which is of great worth in God's sight." (NIV)

THE GRACIOUS WOMAN AND HER RELATIONSHIPS

Chapter Four

CROWN OF HER HUSBAND: The Gracious Wife

"A wife of noble character is her husband's crown..."
(Proverbs 12:4)

THE HIGH AND NOBLE CALLING OF MARRIAGE

While God calls some women to singleness, He calls others to married life. Marriage is a wonderful gift from God to be cultivated, cared for, and celebrated. The Bible even uses marriage as an analogy for God's relationship to His people, and Christ's love for His church. To be married means that God has chosen you to be joined with your husband, and that together the two of you will reflect His image more clearly than you both would alone.

In the beginning, God created a man and then removed one of his ribs to form a woman. The two of them were perfect, and yet somehow incomplete without the other. Each one held a piece of the other. It was only when God brought his two creatures together that they were united as one, and together they reflected the image of God. Marriage brings together a man and woman and unites them as God did at the very beginning. It is, in some mysterious way, a return to creation, to God's original intention for the human race. When sin came into the world, man's first response was to hide himself out of fear and shame. Adam and Eve found fig leaves and sewed them together to cover their vulnerable nakedness. Marriage offers the opportunity to return to God's original intention for an authentic relationship between a man and a woman, living together unashamed and seeing each other as they really are.

There are two Hebrew words for "to know." One word is used for ordinary human relationships. "I know my neighbor Sally." "We know Alice and Bob very well." However, there is another word for "to know," that is *yada*, which is reserved for only two relationships. The first way is used is in describing

> "FINALLY, WE ARE AS WE LOVE. IT IS LOVE THAT MEASURES OUR STATURE."
>
> *William Sloane Coffin*

God's relationship with us. God *knows* us completely and wholly. He knows everything about us, everything we think and feel, what motivates us, what inspires us. Secondly this word is used to describe the intimate relationship between a man and his wife. It is the word used in Genesis 4:1, "And Adam *knew* Eve his wife; and she conceived..." You see, marriage is a deep knowing. It is two people who have surrendered their human tendency towards independence and opened their souls to one another in a lifelong commitment to love, cherish and be totally true to one another.

Marriage can also be an incredible endeavor. It is a furnace for the revolution of the human heart. In some sense, marriage is the ultimate test for how we succeed as human beings, because it challenges our capacity to love and be loved. And yet, love begins rather innocuously. It usually starts in the flutter of a heartbeat and slowly spreads to consume the mind and fill the heart with thoughts of the other person. But love must mature and go from heart palpitations to an unyielding commitment to another. Marriage, in as much as it brings two people together face to face on a daily basis (almost *too* close for comfort) is the breeding ground for true love to become reality. Mike Mason's book *The Mystery of Marriage* describes marriage in this deeply significant way.

> For in the first place, love convinces a couple that they are the greatest romance that has ever been, that no two people have ever loved as they do, and that they will sacrifice absolutely anything to be together. And then marriage asks them to prove it. Marriage is the down-to-earth dimension of romance, the translation of a romantic blueprint into costly reality. It is the practical working out of people's grandest dreams and ideals and promises in the realm of

love. It is one of God's most powerful secret weapons for the revolutionizing of the human heart. It is a heavy, concentrated barrage upon the place of our greatest weakness, which is our relationship with others. We cannot possible, it is true, in any practical way maintain a commitment to every other person in the world: that is God's business, not ours. But marriage involves us synecdochically in this mystical activity of God's by choosing for us just one person, one total stranger out of all the world's billions, with whom to enter into the highest and deepest and farthest reaches of sacrificial, loving relationship.[14]

And so marriage is the deepest, most profound relationship one will ever experience with another human being. It is the confines around which true love is tried and produced. We don't often see it in this light, but marriage is a furnace through which God refines our capacity to love and be loved.

If you are married, your marriage is an integral part of how both you and your husband will fulfill God's call on your lives. We need to recognize the deep significance of marriage and how important it is to embrace our marriages as God-designed. The world sees divorces and unhappy marriages ending all the time, but rarely do people see genuinely happy, enduring marriages. Marriage, as God designed it, is supposed to be a glimpse into heaven itself. When God brings a husband and wife together, their union is supposed to be a reflection of His love and grace to the world.

As a married woman, you are to be a gracious and excellent wife. Proverbs 12:4 tells us that a noble wife is the crown of her husband. She makes her husband shine! In the same way that a crown gives dignity and honor to the person on whose head it rests, a virtuous wife can elevate the reputation of her husband. A gracious wife is one who respects the order of marriage, expresses kindness towards her husband, and sustains the beauty of romance in her marriage.

AN ORDER FOR DANCING

Order is an important principle for gracious living in every area of our lives. It is particularly tangible in personal relationships, and none more so than in marriage. As Christian women we are to love

God first, and then to respect our husbands as God calls us to do. Firstly, we must remember that God is to sit on the throne of our hearts, not our husbands. A husband was never meant to be put on a pedestal, as an idol in the place of God. Now, I know what you're thinking? *Who me? My husband is the last person I would put on a pedestal! He is as human as they come!* That may be true, but sometimes we give our husbands "godlike" status in more subtle ways. We do so by expecting them to fulfill all of our emotional needs. We may have entered marriage with the assumption that marriage will finally complete and satisfy us. We will never feel lonely again. We will always have someone who understands and cares. But the truth is that even the best marriages can not fulfill us completely all the time. There is a place in each person's heart that only the Lord can fill. Blaise Pascal called this our "God-shaped vacuum." St. Augustine understood this as well. He commented, "Our hearts are restless until they rest in Thee." Only God can fulfill us ultimately. If we are seeking constant and perfect completion from our husbands, we will never be entirely satisfied. We will be grasping for what they cannot ultimately fulfill, and our attitude towards our husbands will be needy instead of giving. Instead, we must love God first and through His love, we can operate as truly gracious wives who recognize that God is the ultimate Husband of their souls.

Once we understand the position God should occupy in our hearts, we will also begin to understand the order He desires for each marriage. Marriage should not be a chaotic relationship in which neither partner knows what they should be doing, but one of meaningful order and mutual respect. Many years ago, my husband and I took a few simple dance lessons. Unfortunately, it didn't last long because I am the bearer of a dominant "klutz gene". But what we did learn was that in every dance, one leads and another follows. If you could have two leaders in a dance, you would end up going in two separate directions and never find yourself in step with one another. One leads, and the other follows and complements the lead. Each play unique and equally valuable roles, but their roles are a bit different. That is the idea of order in a marriage. A husband has a unique role in a marriage and so does a wife.

The Bible teaches that wives are to be submitted to our husbands. I Peter 3:1-2 instructs wives to "…be submissive to your husbands so that, if any of them do not believe the word, they may be won over without words by the behavior of their wives, when they see the purity and reverence of your lives." To many women, submission is an uncomfortable word with outdated notions of a wife in an apron pandering to her husband's every beck and call. Christian submission is never supposed to be a form of modern-day slavery or an excuse for abuse. Rather, Biblical submission begins first with submitting ourselves to God's authority in our lives. In fact, *both* husband and wife are to submit their lives firstly to God. As they both allow God to take the reigns of their hearts, they will display godly character towards each other. God calls husbands to display Christ-like, sacrificial leadership in their families[15], and wives to support them in their roles as leaders in the home. Becoming a gracious wife means developing a gentle and quiet spirit that seeks to honor and respect our husbands as they endeavor to become the servant leaders God calls them to be.

A woman's encouragement and confidence can make a world of difference for a man's self-esteem and ability to lead. Although many men appear self-assured and impenetrable on the outside, inside they may still retain the heart of a little boy who is looking for approval and acceptance from others. That is why a woman's respect and support are so important to a man. She strengthens him and empowers him to become a better person. She gives him the courage he needs to be the leader he is called to be. On the other hand, a woman's disdain and ridicule can have disastrous effects on a man's sense of who he is and even on his masculinity. I don't think we as women often realize the power that our words and attitudes have on the men in our lives. We sometimes believe it is our duty to correct them, when in fact, they most need our comfort and consolation. A man will change for a woman, but more often than not, he will respond to a woman's gentleness and honest vulnerability rather than her harsh and critical words, however true they may be.

Sometimes a wife feels she must function as the role of the Holy Spirit in her husband's life. She constantly reminds him what he should be doing, how he can be a better Christian, better father, better provider…. while carefully scrutinizing (and pointing out) areas needing improvement. I know I am guilty of being a "spiritual" nag to my husband at times. There have been days when it isn't 30 seconds from the time his foot steps in the door until he is met with my laundry list of personal grievances! While there is certainly a place for speaking the truth in love to our husbands, part of respecting and submitting to our husbands is waiting to speak that truth at the appropriate time (and occasionally, not to say anything at all!) That is what these verses from I Peter 3 are trying to tell us. Sometimes our husbands are won over not by our carefully crafted words, but by our godly behavior and quiet respect and trust. It takes great faith to trust God to work in our husbands' lives, and to realize that God may not really need our help at all. Sometimes we may even hinder our husband's ability to hear God because we are so busy talking to him instead!

And so, order plays an important role in woman's ability to love her husband and to be the gracious wife she is called to be. Firstly, a woman must remember her first love, that is her relationship with God, and keep it supreme in her heart. By rightly honoring God and looking to Him to meet her needs, a woman can become a giving and loving wife. Then, by respecting the order with which God designed marriage, she can encourage and honor the leadership of her husband. This is the first step towards a truly gracious marriage!

What Kindness Does to a Man

While charm and physical beauty may attract a man's attention, a woman's kindness is what makes an indelible impression on his soul. Kindness touches a man on the inside in a profound way. A wife's kindness not only heals and comforts her husband's heart, but is an extension of God's grace in a marriage. As every marriage has conflict and hurt, so every marriage needs kindness. A wife who shows kindness to her husband is one who will inevitably be called upon to forgive her husband when he has hurt her, and in her act of forgiveness, she has stepped above the human equations of "give and take" and into God's way of mercy and grace. A few years ago, a couple we had known for years began having serious marital troubles. He and his wife were going through counseling with a professional therapist and the therapist asked both of them to list what hurts and grievances each had with the other. When they came back the next week, the husband had written out about two sentences on his paper, and the wife had filled five full sheets of lined paper with grievances. She had not forgiven him for things he had done to hurt her all the way back to when they were first married. Now I am sure that many of the things she listed were justified, but at some point, she was still going to have to forgive her husband if she wanted her marriage to succeed.

Forgiveness is a willing relinquishment of certain rights. The one sinned against chooses *not* to demand her rights of redress for the hurt she has suffered. She does not hold her spouse accountable for his sin, nor enforce a punishment upon him, nor exact a payment from him, as in "reparations." She does not make his life miserable in order to balance accounts for her own misery, though she might feel perfectly justified in doing so... In this way she steps *outside* the systems of law; she steps *into* the world of mercy. She makes possible a whole new economy for their relationship: not the cold-blooded machinery of rules, rights and privileges, but the tender and nourishing care of mercy, which always rejoices in the growth, not the guilt or the pain, of the other. This is sacrifice. To give up one's rights is to sacrifice something of one's self – something hard-fought-for in the world.[16]

Besides being an expression of God's grace, kindness, particularly when a woman shows kindness to a man, can be an expression of a woman's uniquely feminine nature. A woman's greatest strength is in her softness, her ability to nurture, her gentle compassion. Men are not only deeply attracted to kindness in a woman, but it inspires them to become the strong, godly men they were designed to be. A feminine woman makes a man want to become more masculine. When a man is around a feminine, gentle woman, he is inspired to grow in strength of character, to become a protector and provider. We as modern women, particularly those of us who are highly educated and achieved professional success, sometimes view femininity as a weakness. But the truth is that our feminine nature is a strength, and kindness and gentleness, not forceful words and clever arguments, have the greatest power to transform a man's heart. So don't be afraid to be a true woman and allow your kindness and unique feminine nature to inspire your husband's heart.

Fyodor Dostoevsky, in his novel *Crime and Punishment*, creates such a woman as his heroine. His protagonist is a man named Raskolnikov, and commits a cold-blooded murder at the beginning of the narrative. But immediately afterwards, he becomes anguished and full of guilt and panic. The novel follows him through the aftermath of his criminal act and his eventual redemption. When he meets Sonia, a prostitute who has sacrificed herself for her family's survival, he confesses his crime to her. She does not condemn him but offers him unconditional love, while also encouraging him to confess to the authorities. It is through her gentle spirit and unfaltering support that he eventually confesses, faces imprisonment, and finds God's redemption. That is what a woman's kindness can do to a man. It empowers him to reach heights in himself that he could not have aimed for without her and to become a better man.

Finally, a gracious wife can show kindness to her husband by keeping a positive attitude. Gary Smalley, in his book *For Better or For Best: Understand Your Man* lists certain qualities that men find uniquely attractive in a woman. Besides a gentle spirit and an ability to communicate respect, men were uniquely attracted to a woman's positive attitude.[17] Being cheerful and pleasant isn't always the first thing that one thinks of as a way to be kind to someone, but it is. How many times have you met a stranger who was gloomy and curt and even though you had nothing to do with why she was feeling the way she was, you left feeling hurt and dejected yourself? We don't always realize it, but our moods have a great impact on everyone around us.

A man is drawn to and energized by a woman's positive attitude and calm, gentle spirit. We have the ability to lift our husband's spirit as soon as he walks through the door. Likewise, our complaining and negativity can sour his mood as well as our entire household! Even the Bible has something to say about a quarrelsome wife. It tells us that a man would

> ✑✑
>
> "WOMEN ARE A BLESSING TO EVERY CIRCLE IN WHICH THEY MOVE, IF THEY WILL BUT CULTIVATE A CHEERFUL, HAPPY, BLITHESOME DISPOSITION."
>
> *Daisy Eyebright*
>
> ✑✑

rather live in the corner of the roof than to share a house with a wife who is always nagging and complaining.[18] Don't drive your husband away with a negative spirit. Rather, keep a positive outlook and you will soon learn what it means to have a magnetic personality! People like being around brightness and joy.

Daisy Eyebright, in her famed Victorian

manual of etiquette quipped that, "A pleasant, cheerful wife is as a rainbow, set in the sky, when her husband's mind is beset with storms and tempests; but a dissatisfied and fretful wife, in the hour of trouble, is like one of those fiends who are appointed to torture the lost spirits."[19] It is a little dramatic, but the point is that your kindness and sweetness is like a beacon of light for which your husband looks to you. Let your light shine brightly.

REKINDLING THE BEAUTY OF ROMANCE

Finally, a gracious wife is one that keeps alive the beauty of romance in her marriage. Romance is to marriage what beauty is to a woman. It is that extra sparkle, the thing that makes a marriage glow. A marriage is bound to grow and change throughout its lifetime, and although it becomes easy to focus on our children, our careers, our homes and other things, we must make an effort to keep romance alive in our marriages.

Romance comes naturally to most couples at

the start of a marriage. Husbands remember holidays and buy flowers and gifts. Wives look for ways to surprise their husbands with special meals and planned outings. But frequently, after a couple has been married for a few years (and especially after having children), romance is often set aside along with the likes of holding the door open for each other. Who has time or energy enough for romance? Besides, we may tell ourselves, love is not romance, and we should not expect our marriage to maintain the same feelings we had when we were dating. That is true, we will not feel the same way we did towards our spouses five or ten years into a marriage. On the contrary, our love should be stronger and our feelings richer and deeper!

Romance is something that we should cultivate throughout marriage and adds value to a loving marriage. The main elements of romance are creativity, variety, and surprise. And it doesn't have to be overly complicated or time-consuming. It can be as simple as mailing a card to your husband's office. Or tucking a small present into his briefcase.

You could invite him to a mid-week movie night. After the kids are asleep, you pop the popcorn, and he gets to pick the movie. It doesn't really matter so much what you do, but just that you do it. Any little act of romance tells your husband that he is important to you and that you still enjoy his company.

Finally, as you keep the beauty of romance alive in your marriage, don't forget to keep yourself beautiful! Do you remember how beautiful your husband thought you were when he first met you? It is easy to get sloppy about your physical appearance, especially around your husband. After all, he sees you when you first wake up, with no makeup, frizzy hair and bad breath! Don't allow your physical appearance to go just because he sees you in your worst imaginable state. He also needs to see you at your best. Remember that your husband isn't expecting you to be a supermodel. He married *you* and thinks *you* are beautiful, so be the very best version of yourself that you can be! You can become the most beautiful woman in the world, in the eyes of your own husband, by meeting his deepest needs as a man and by becoming the kind of gracious woman who will continue to inspire and captivate him.

A LOVE THAT LASTS

As we grow in becoming gracious women, we should aim for truly gracious marriages, ones that are rooted in unconditional love, in God's great love for us. Most of us begin "loving" each other based on conditions. When we started dating, our husbands were handsome and charming and strong. They made us feel special and did nice things for us. We didn't realize it then, but our love was somewhat conditional. As our marriage grows, our love should become more and more unconditional, not based on what we do for one another, but based on the unconditional, boundless love of God. Our love for our husbands should be constant, not easily changed by our emotions or experiences.

As a marriage deepens, love must actively grow and increase with the movement of our lives. Elisabeth Elliot wrote, "Love is dynamic, not static." Unconditional love means that we love our husbands *through* life's unexpected changes, and *in spite* of the changes that may never come. That is why marriage begins with promises. When each of us married we spoke very serious vows before God and by God's grace and the power of the Holy Spirit in us, we can keep those promises. Elisabeth Elliot, in her book *Let Me Be a Woman* wrote:

> Your provider may someday lose his job. Your strength may show unexpected weakness. Your knight in shining armor may experience a public defeat. Your teacher may make a mistake that you tried to warn him about. Your lover may become a helpless patient, sick, sore, and sad, needing your presence and care every minute of the day and night. 'This isn't the man I married,' you will say, and it will be true. But you married him for better or for worse, in sickness and in health, and those tremendous promises took into account the possibility of radical change. That's why promises were necessary.[20]

But do not despair at the overwhelming seriousness of those promises. The grace of God that allowed you to make such promises in the first place is also enough to keep you true to them. Ultimately, we see that true love begins and ends with God. He is the orchestrator of love and marriage and He is sustainer of true and abiding love.

SINGLE AND COMPLETE

Finally, I would like to end this chapter on marriage with a few words about singleness. Although God calls some women to marriage, He does not call *all* women into marriage. And the truth is that all married women will spend some portion of their lives single, either before they marry or after a spouse passes away, or in some cases, after an unfortunate divorce. Whether a woman is single for a portion of her life or single for all of her life, singleness is not a lesser state than marriage. A woman is made complete not by a man, but by God. She can be whole and fulfilled as a single woman. Being single successfully means to be a whole person.[21] Some women are even called to remain single life in order to live a fully devoted life to God and to serving others. I Corinthians 7:34 tells us that "An unmarried woman or virgin is concerned about the Lord's affairs: Her aim is to be devoted to the

Lord in both body and spirit. But a married woman is concerned about the affairs of this world--how she can please her husband." A single woman has a capacity to focus wholeheartedly and single-mindedly on God without much of the concerns that married women carry. In fact, some of the greatest women of God were single. Women like Amy Carmichael and Mother Theresa lived singly devoted to His purposes. In the freedom of their state, they went where many married women could not, and accomplished much for the kingdom of God.

For some, being single may be a time of preparation for marriage. God may be molding and developing your character as well as that of your future spouse, and at the perfect time, He will bring you together. Use your time as a single woman to grow in your relationship with the Lord, to develop those character traits and skills necessary to be successful in marriage.

For all single women, single life will sometimes involve times of loneliness and solitude. It takes faith, fortitude and the fellowship of good friends to help you through those times. It also helps to live your life with purpose, understanding the Lord's will for you and trusting Him to complete the good work He began in you. Try to have this perspective through times of loneliness, and you will learn how to experience God during those times. Ingrid Trobisch was the wife of Walter Trobisch, a missionary teacher and writer. When her husband passed away, she had to re-learn the art of being alone.

> ....I learned to fill up those alone times. Anyone who enjoys reading never needs to stay lonely, because by reading you can get in touch with great minds and share their thoughts. Sometimes I did handiwork. I have a needlepoint cushion top that went around the world with me three times before I finished it, but it helped me when I could neither read nor write. I play the piano – not very well – but I am often helped by singing or learning the words of a new hymn. Loneliness can be gift from God. It can be His magnet to draw us to Him. He made us capable of great loneliness to ensure that we don't stagnate and that we reach beyond ourselves to Him, to new experiences, to other people, people who need us because they are lonely too.[22]

Married or single, we are called to be wholly fulfilled women. We are called to say yes to who God has created us to be, and to live fully alive in the destiny he has given us. We are called to be gracious women.

REFLECT AND RESPOND

1. Read I Corinthians 13:1-13. How is love described in this chapter? In what way can you show love to your husband?

2. How has your marriage changed through the years? Are there areas you and your husband could work on together? Spend some time together and talk honestly about your hopes and disappointments. Pray together as a couple.

3. Surprise your husband by planning something romantic.

4. Memorize I Corinthians 13:4-7. "Love is patient, love is kind. It does not envy, it does not boast, it is not proud. It is not rude, it is not self-seeking, it is not easily angered, it keeps no record of wrongs. Love does not delight in evil but rejoices with the truth. It always protects, always trusts, always hopes, always perseveres." (NIV)

Chapter Five

BEARER OF LIFE:
The Gracious Mother

"Her children arise and call her blessed…"
(Proverbs 31:28)

THE CALL OF MOTHERHOOD

Women have one of the greatest privileges in life, that of bearing and raising children. God designed women with the amazing capacity to bear a child, bring him into this world and even nourish him physically for a time. Although not every woman will marry or bear children, a woman's physical and emotional makeup still attests to the marvelous ability she has to nurture and care for children. Women have been designed and called to motherhood and all its wonderful joy and complexity.

As a mother, you have the tremendous task of not only bringing a child *into* the world, but preparing him *for* the world. It is an awesome responsibility and joy to raise a child, to nurture and teach him, to encourage him to become all that God has destined him to be. A mother's love and influence on a child in her early years has an impact that remains throughout her entire life and even for eternity. History is replete with examples of mothers who have influenced their children in powerful ways. Susanna Wesley, often called the "Mother of Methodism" had a profound impact on the lives of her famous sons, John and Charles Wesley. She spent individualized time with each of her children, teaching them about God and John and Charles went on to win tens of thousands of souls for Christ. Mary Washington, mother of the first President of the United States, raised her children bravely. Widowed at 35 years of age, she continued to manage the family farm as well as care for her own children. George Washington said of her, "My mother was the most beautiful woman I ever saw. All I am I owe to my mother. I attribute all my success in life to the moral, intellectual and physical education I received from her."

Mothers have a unique connection with their children which is established very early. Studies have been shown that even babies in-utero have the

> ෫෧ ෧෨
> "ALL THAT I AM OR EVER HOPE TO BE, I OWE TO MY ANGEL MOTHER."
>
> *Abraham Lincoln*
>
> ෫෧ ෧෨

ability to distinguish their mother's voice from that of a stranger. Cradled in their mother's womb for months, a baby spends all day listening to his mother's voice: when she talks to others, talks to him, sings to herself. When researchers in China played tape recordings of a poem read by various women, the fetuses responded with quickened heart rates when they heard their own mothers' voices. Their heart rates decreased when they heard the voice of strangers.[23] In fact, a newborn baby's sense of hearing is developed before her sense of sight, and often turns in the direction of her mother when she hears her voice. God has given mothers a unique ability to speak into their children's lives. Her voice is the first one a child hears and often continues to be a source of wisdom, comfort and instruction throughout life.

A mother's influence is far reaching. Just as a mother's body actually provides the nutrients needed for her unborn baby, so her faithful prayers, counsel and godly example will sustain them as they grow into maturity. Because a child's relationship with his mother is the first relationship he will have, it is often the lens through which he judges the world and others. A child picks up his mother's language, her accent and mannerisms. He learns to read her emotions and reactions; he discovers what in the world is safe, what is acceptable, what is funny, what is fearful. She teaches him not only numbers and letters, but guides his spiritual and moral development. When you stop and think of how foundational a child's first few years of life are, it makes you realize what an awesome privilege and task you have as a mother.

The fascinating thing is that this magnificent calling and the unique position you have as a mother works itself out in the routine, daily happenings of life. The fabric of your relationship with your children is woven in the seemingly mundane and trivial acts that you perform every day as a mother. The young mom who changes diapers and cleans up after her toddler all day long is already in the process of developing a relationship with her child. Although it may seem ordinary, the kindness she shows now and the trust she develops during play time become the foundation of what kind of relationship they will have as the child grows. The reason her teenage daughter can talk to her about her problems is only because they have grown a relationship over time that begins in early childhood.

God has called us as moms to be gracious ones, mothers who impact their children's hearts for eternity. Be the kind of gracious woman that your children will be proud of, the kind of mother they will one day arise and call blessed. The three key principles of gracious living can be applied to becoming a gracious mother. A gracious mother is one who brings godly order into her children's lives, affects their hearts with kindness and inspires their imaginations with beauty.

ORDER OUT OF CHAOS

Among the many things a mother provides her children is the shelter of an ordered world. Although they may not admit it, children need order in their lives. And this order comes in many forms. All mothers of young children know how important it is for a child to have a reasonable routine for their day. When naptime and mealtimes are delayed or skipped, temper tantrums and meltdowns often follow. As children get older, they still need order in their home routine. Mothers of children at all stages can provide this order by planning their daily schedules appropriately and not overloading children with too much activity. Children and adults all need "downtime" and moms can carve out time in each day to give their children restful time for them to pursue their own leisure and hobbies.

Secondly, order means that children have reasonable, age-appropriate boundaries which are consistently enforced. Children need for the rules and expectations of their home to be clearly explained to them. They shouldn't have to wonder what the rules of their home are, and they should not be expected to follow rules that are made up as they go. Family rules should be understandable. A child should be able to repeat them back to her parents in such a way to show that she understands what is expected of her. Children should also know what the potential consequences for overstepping those boundaries are. And those consequences should be appropriate to the infraction. Discipline should not be meted out haphazardly or in the heat of an emotional battle of wills. It should be an expected and logical consequence of willfully breaking a rule.

An ordered world is also one of emotional order. Children need emotionally stable and healthy parents. It is unsettling and scary for children to be in a home where one or both parents are unable to control their tempers, or manage their emotions. A gracious mother must have control over her own emotions, words and behavior so that she can provide the emotional security and stability her children need.

When my oldest son was very young, we often battled over eating. One of our battles was over his drinking too much of juice, which of course all toddlers innately prefer over water or milk. One evening, around 3 in the morning, he woke up screaming for juice. I was exhausted and a bit fed up at fighting with him over this issue and decided in my own mind that I was finally going to win this battle of wills. Well, my son had a will to match mine, and we continued for about an hour going back and forth. I got him water. He refused it. I got him milk. He continued screaming and crying. Finally, I was so furious that I got up and started yelling at him and finally slammed his bedroom door. As I slammed the door on his beet-red face, still screaming for juice, It dawned on me that I was acting just like my two-year old. I was having a temper tantrum that looked curiously like his. Since that time, I have become convinced that motherhood and discipline is often more about self-control than about controlling the behavior of my children. My children don't gain anything from seeing their mother barking out orders or threatening time-outs at them. They need a mother who is poised and ordered in her own heart and soul, so that they can learn how to have order in their own lives.

Finally, children need to have relational order in their lives. They need a mother who has a proper view of herself and a proper view of her marriage. Long before a mother ever became a mom, she was a person loved by her Creator and created for His pleasure. A mother's first priority should be to her God and all that He calls her to be, which will inevitably make her a better mother. Secondly, her priority should be to her husband. She is a wife before she is a mother. One of the best things a mother can do for her children is to love and respect their father, and to give priority to her marriage when needed.

Something unusual seems to happen somewhere between the positive pregnancy test and the midnight diaper changes. I never thought I would struggle with this before I became a mother. I had read books and heard numerous sermons about how parents should put their marriage ahead of the demands of parenthood. I understood in my head that children should not become an emotional substitute for a healthy marriage. But as soon as I gave birth to my first son, my world was turned upside down! All of a sudden, a new man had entered my life. Although he was less than 2 feet tall and couldn't utter a word, he was my pint-sized Prince Charming! I soon found myself giving all of my time and energy to the portly little fellow. While there are certainly practical reasons why mothers spend more time with their children, especially when they are young, the temptation for many women is that even when their children are older, we see ourselves primarily as mothers and secondarily as wives. This is particularly challenging as an all-the-time-at-home mom. It is so easy to let my children become my entire world. After all, I enjoy them and I find purpose and meaning in being their mother. But I need to constantly remind myself and ask God to help me put motherhood in its rightful place, which is second to my marriage. It is best for the entire family, not only for husband and wife, but for the children. Children gain great personal and social security in knowing that Mom and Dad love each other. They also learn that the family does not revolve around their needs, but around the core nucleus, namely Mom and Dad. So, keep motherhood in its proper position. It seems a little counterintuitive but you will actually be a better mother by choosing not to see yourself *primarily* as a mother but as a wife first.

Being a gracious mother starts with providing your children with an ordered world. Children need order for their proper growth and development. Keep a consistent schedule that fits their age and needs. Manage your own emotions so that they will have the security of a stable home. And finally, keep relational order in your role as a mother. Be a Christian first and keep God as first in your heart. Your children will respect how you live your life as you trust God in putting Him first. Then, you are a wife and next a mother. In this way, you will be providing your children a little bit of necessary order out of chaos.

BE KIND TO TENDER HEARTS

Sometimes I feel like my primary duty as a mother is to change the behavior of my children. After all, I spend a great portion of my day repeating such commands as, "Finish your meal," "Clean up your toys," and "Don't fight with your brother." For many moms, especially those with young children, much of our energy is consumed by trying to "coerce" our children into socially acceptable behavior. After all, we all suspect that our children's obedience or disobedience (particularly in public) somehow proves to others our success or failure as moms.

As our children get older, we may shift our focus towards shaping their minds and teaching them how to think about the world around them. For homeschooling mothers, we are literally educating them in all subjects that they will need as they enter higher education and adulthood. All mothers look for teachable moments to move their children towards a God-centered, biblical worldview. While changing behavior and educating minds are important, neither should not be the primary goal of a mother. A mother's mission is far deeper and important: to cultivate a child's heart towards faith in God. It is a child's heart (what truly excites him, what moves him from the inside) that will chart the course of his life. After all, given enough promise of reward or threat of punishment, most children can mimic good behavior. With enough teaching and memorization, most children can recite all of the right facts and "doctrinal" statements. But the heart is an entirely different matter. Proverbs 4:23 tell us that the heart is the wellspring of life. Everything, good and bad, flows out of the heart and it is what charts the course of a child's life and transition into adulthood.

Therefore, the mission of a gracious mother is to love her children towards Christ and cultivate the seeds of faith she plants in their tender hearts. The true character of a Christian mother is tested in the home, where she is most herself, and able to be as mean or as kind as she truly is. St. Francis of Assisi was attributed with the saying, "Preach the Gospel at all times. Use words if necessary." That is especially true when it comes to our life at home. Children, particularly young ones, are very impressionable and absorb almost everything from the people they spend their days with. That is why we need to be kind and show our children an transparent Christian life.

Children will see and imitate their mother's actions and her reactions to what happens in ordinary, everyday life more than they listen to the words she uses to teach them. Children know how their parents truly live and can easily detect hypocrisy. No amount of family devotions or Bible instruction can cover up a poor living example. This doesn't mean that we have to be perfect. As mothers, we all make mistakes. Children don't need a sinless example of a Christian to know God's love. They need for their mothers to be authentic and willing to admit fault when wrong and ask forgiveness when they have hurt them.

The best place for a child to learn about God's love is in the home. Your kindness and compassion towards your children is a tangible expression of the unconditional, immeasurable love of God. Tender little hearts need to be told regularly and shown consistently how much they are loved. Give your children hugs frequently. Spend time doing things they enjoy. Moms of young children know how much their children enjoy what I call "floor time," sitting on the floor playing with their toys. Focus your full attention on your children when they are talking to you. All of these seemingly small acts of love show your children how much God loves them. A mother's unconditional love is also the anchor on which a child's self esteem rests. As children go out into the world, they will be bombarded with messages about how others view them and how they measure up when compared with their peers. As children attempt to define themselves in this shaky new ground, their minds will return to the messages that have been told about themselves. A mother is a key factor in how a child views herself. Proverbs 18:21 tells us that "the tongue has the power of life and death." The words that come out of a mother's mouth have the power to bless or curse her children. Use your words to bless and affirm your children's worth in God's eyes. Encourage your children and tell them how much they are loved and valued.

A mother can use words of blessing even when disciplining her child. Focusing on the positive and believing in a child gives him the ability to obey his parents and do well. A mother can react to a child's disobedience in two ways. She can focus on the negative by saying, "Johnny, what in the world were you thinking? How could you be so foolish? You will never amount to anything if you keep messing up like that." Or she can say, "Johnny, what you did was wrong, but I know you can do better than that." One reaction not only scolds the action, but also blames the child. The other response addresses the problem while also offering hope for the child to improve.

Even adults tend to thrive or fail under the expressed expectations that they sense from others. When placed under a boss who is looking for an excuse to fire you, you will inevitably find yourself making mistakes and unable to perform in the way you normally would. But when you are in an environment where your boss is excited to have you on staff and sees an unlimited potential in you, you will naturally improve and enjoy the process of growth as well. In the same way, a child will behave better and learn quicker in a home where her parents believe in her and hope the best for her, and not one in which she feels like she is always under surveillance, being watched for the next mistake.

As you express kindness to your children, be sure that you communicate a love that is unconditional. If a mother praises her child only when he obeys or "performs" in some way, she is potentially setting him up to become a perfectionist who believes his self worth is based on his performance. Express love to your children on a regular basis, regardless of whether they have brought home a good grade or cleaned their rooms. They should know that your love will always be there, even if they fail at what they do.

Every child is different and a wise and gracious mother understands the unique temperament in her children and expresses kindness in a way appropriate to each child. How does your child experience love? Does he most appreciate the time you spend with him one on one? Does she love receiving gifts? My love language has always been gifts and somehow my mother really understood this. She was wonderful at surprising me with small gifts, often undeserved and not for any particular occasion. I still remember as a young girl, opening up my school desk and discovering a sheet of pretty stickers inside and a note that said, "I love you." She had been at a parent-teacher conference the night before and tucked them into my desk so I could find them the next day. I felt overwhelmed by my mother's kindness and thoughtfulness. Later in my life, I came to know Christ through her witness and prayers for me. My mother had laid the foundation for an understanding of God's unconditional love through her kindness and her imperfect (but honest) example of what it meant to live a Christian life at home. Now that I have children of my own, I pray that I will likewise understand their uniquely shaped needs and be a conduit for God's unconditional love to them.

INSPIRE IMAGINATION WITH BEAUTY

The third component of gracious living
is beauty, and one way that a gracious mother can
teach her children to appreciate what is truly beautiful
in this world by inspiring their imaginations towards
creativity. Children today are offered a plethora of
television shows and video games that make it easy
for them to passively pass the time instead of actively
engaging their imagination in creative play. Try to
offer your children alternatives to passive leisure so
that they can exercise their bodies and minds through
discovery, learning and creative thinking.

Children of the past were content to play with
very simple toys: wooden blocks, trains, dolls and
coloring books. Somehow, their imagination made
these simple things come alive and become
sufficiently entertaining. Today, we have a plethora
of toys, with bells and whistles all competing to
sustain our children's attention. Many of the toys
today are character toys marketed alongside movies or

television shows. Toys of the past were tools in the hands of creative little children. We leave very little to plain old-fashioned make-believe anymore, but I believe that all children are capable of imaginative play. Encourage your children to play pretend and create their own adventures, build their own structures, even make their own toys!

Keeping a stock of art and craft supplies at home is also a great way to encourage creativity. Children need only a few simple instructions to begin creating their next masterpiece. They love working with their hands and take pride in showing off their completed works of art! Make sure you display their masterpieces. There are lots of creative ways to showcase your children's artwork around the house. Besides the traditional magnets on the refrigerator, you can use clothes pins and hang them across a wire against a wall. You can put them on decorative small easels. And everything always looks like a masterpiece when you put it in a frame. Consider getting a simple brass nameplate engraved with your child's name. You can easily switch out the drawing as she gets older and wants to change it. Take your children to museums and introduce them to fine art. Buy them books that teach them about art.

Introduce your children to the beauty of music. There are so many different kinds of music to learn about, and many ways to teach your children to appreciate music. Our city orchestra has a quarterly classical music concert for kids. They have a "musical petting zoo" before the concert where kids can handle and try out all sorts of instruments. The concert is only about 45 minutes and they make it engaging and interactive for young children. When my children were younger, I took them to a Mommy and Me music class. Each week, the children would play with musical toys and learn about different styles of music from around the world. As they got older, we took them to the symphony. Keeping music on in your home and car is also a great way to sneak in some music appreciation.

Reading and listening to stories are also great ways to cultivate the imagination and a love of learning. Keep a good variety of books all over your house. Let your children pick out their own books for you to read to them. Many libraries and bookstores have children's story time for young children. As they are able to read on their own, talk about books with your children. Continue reading with your children even as they grow. Some families have evening "read aloud" story time and each member of the family reads a passage from a book. Introduce your children to wholesome film adaptations of their favorite novels. Excite them about reading.

Taking your kids outdoors is also a great way for children to exercise both their minds and their bodies. Young children love exploring. Give them magnifying glasses and have them look for bugs and flowers in the yard. Take them on nature walks. Collect interesting specimens. Press leaves and flowers from your walks. Send them on a scavenger hunt with a little treasure at the end. Give your children sidewalk chalk and bubbles to blow. Go for family bike rides. Breathe fresh air together and marvel at God's creation.

Another way you can inspire your children's imagination is to create beautiful, child-friendly spaces for them in the home. I love decorating rooms and cozy nooks in our home around things that my children love and will be inspired to play around. When we transitioned my oldest son to sleeping on a bed, we decided not to get a bed with safety rails. Instead, we opted for a soft foam mattress that went directly on the floor. That way, when he rolled over, he would be only inches from the ground. Well, it was not the most attractive thing to have a mattress stuck on the floor. So I designed his room around the idea of "camping out" in the jungle. Soon, his simple mattress became an outdoor hideaway in the midst of a safari of palm trees and jungle animals. We had safari stuffed animals, I created life-size jungle animals on the walls and hung hooks where he could keep a safari hat and homemade "binoculars" (two toilet paper rolls glued together and tied with yarn) for him to go on his own adventures. To top it off, he had his own safari play tent with a secret tunnel that only he and his brother could fit through!

To encourage reading, I turned an unused corner of our upstairs bonus room into a "kid-sized" book nook. All it took was low-lying bookcase where the children's books were easily accessible and attractively displayed, a thick fluffy rug and pillows perfect for cuddling up to. And most importantly, I made sure to spend personal time with the kids, reading to them and just sitting with them as they read books of their own.

There are so many ways to add beauty into your children's lives. And the best part is that as you think of ways to inspire your children's imagination, you will find your own imagination brimming with new ideas and creative projects to pursue. You too may get to relive and enjoy a little bit of your own childhood once again!

A MOTHER'S REWARD

Like anything worth doing, motherhood can also be hard work at times. It can be difficult navigating through the demands of daily life and the expectations we put on ourselves. Mothers are often juggling various responsibilities: being a wife, caring for the home, serving in the church, working an outside job. But among the greatest achievements a woman can have in life is raising a future generation of children who will love and serve God with all their hearts. Your impact on the lives of your children not only has an effect on your family, but future generations and on the world they touch. The funny thing is that this tremendous undertaking we have as mothers is not made up of grand accomplishments, but of small, everyday, ordinary moments. It is the little kindnesses that we show to our children in caring for them every day that add up to the wonder of motherhood.

As I look back on my own life, the one person that I have to thank the most for leading me to Christ is my mother. She did not win me to Christ with an eloquent, forceful testimony. Although she faithfully lead us in devotions and taught us about the Bible, it wasn't the lessons she taught us that meant the most. It was those times I remember waking up in the middle of the night afraid and stumbling over to her bedroom where she always responded to my little tugs. As tired as she was, she always rose and took me to the kitchen where she poured me a glass of milk and sat there with me until we finished it. I don't remember what we talked about then, or if we said anything at all. But to this day, it is the kindness of those little acts that made her a trustworthy and sincere witness to the love of God.

Finally, as a mother, perhaps the best thing you can do for your children is simply to pray for them. No one will pray for your children with the fervency and devotion that you will pray for them. And when all is said and done, our efforts to teach and train and love them, will all fall short without the sustaining love and grace of God. I often reflect on how little I can really do for my children. Ultimately, I can only depend on God to protect and develop my children in ways that I can only pray for. But I trust that He is faithful. As it says in Philippians 1:3-6, "I thank my God every time I remember you. In all my prayers for all of you, I always pray with joy because of your partnership in the gospel from the first day until now, being confident of this, that he who began a good work in you will carry it on to completion until the day of Christ Jesus." May God bring to completion in our children all the work we do as mothers!

Reflect and Respond

1. Reflect on your relationship with your children. Are you the kind of mother that your children will look up to with honor?

2. Susanna Wesley, a homeschooling mother of ten, made a special weekly appointment with each of her children for one-on-one encouragement and spiritual instruction. Try to carve out a special time for individual "just mommy and me" talk. It can consist of reading a story, having an exchange of "question and answer" time or having a short devotional and prayer together. Whatever activity you do together, the most important thing you can give them is your full attention and time. You will be building the bonds of lasting trust and openness.

3. What are each of your children's love languages? What can you do this week to show kindness to each of your children in a way that they will most appreciate?

4. Commit to praying for your children every day. Be specific and list at least 3 things that you can pray about for each child.

5. Memorize Proverbs 31:28 "Her children arise and call her blessed…"

Chapter Six

KEEPER OF TRUST:
The Gracious Friend

"A friend loves at all times..."
(Proverbs 17:17)

THE VALUE OF A GOOD FRIEND

Good friendships are among the most valuable things in life. Friends make life experiences more meaningful and the trials of life less difficult. They can encourage you in your faith, pray for you, and help you through hard times. When life is difficult and we wonder if God has abandoned us, our friends can restore our faith and give us hope. We can even experience God's presence through our friends.

A friend is someone to whom I do not have to explain myself. Such a friendship offers unspeakable comfort. Friendships can also be redemptive, for friends can act as mediators of God's presence and invite us into the embrace of God's grace.[24]

Friendship is one of the primary ways that God uses us as instruments of His grace. A few years ago, a couple in our Bible study group, finally got pregnant after experiencing years of infertility. We all believed it to be the Lord's answer to prayer. But nine months later, their full term baby girl was delivered stillborn. In their deep sorrow, they questioned God and wondered where He was in the tragic situation. But as several of her friends rallied around her, Natalie and her husband began to sense the presence of God once again. God was not silent because He was not silent in us.

The last two chapters have looked at a gracious woman's relationships with her husband and children, a woman's role as a wife and mother. As we move outside the circle of a woman's closest relationships at home, we come to a woman's friendships. In most of a woman's other relationships, whether it is as a neighbor, sister or daughter-in-law, her role is to be a friend. Women are called to be friends in almost every sphere in which they move!

As gracious women, we are called to be true and faithful friends. But women don't always have the best reputation for friendship. We have been known to gossip, compete with and betray one another. We are often petty and dramatic. Many of us have been burned by our friendships with other women. Who among us hasn't felt the pain of being passed over by a friend who is suddenly closer with another friend? As we grow in Christ, His love will heal those hurts from past friendships and give us the grace to become the faithful friends we are called to be.

God calls us as Christian women to be confidants, trustworthy keepers of secrets and loyal vessels that carry God's grace in each and every friendship. We each have the potential to be blessings to our friends. Our words, prayers and even just our presence can make all the difference in the world for someone. In order to be gracious friends, we must make friendship a priority and make time for it in our lives. We must also remember that kindness is a necessary ingredient in all true friendships. And we can bring beauty into the lives of our friends by sharing ourselves and the things which inspire us.

MAKE TIME FOR FRIENDSHIPS

I think the older we get, the harder it is to make new friends. Life has a way of getting so busy that we feel like we can't give any extra time to invest in new friends, or keep up old friendships. Sometimes I feel like I hardly have time to cultivate a good relationship with my husband and children, much less anyone else outside of my immediate circle of family ties. I also find that it is easy to miss opportunities for new friendships because I am not looking for them. But taking the time to develop and sustain friendships is important. Ordering your life to make friendship a priority means not only opening up your calendar but also your heart to people. Even in our very busy age, it is possible to make room for friendship, and when done, it is also deeply rewarding.

There are lots of ways to get to develop new friendships and deepen old ones. The most important thing is to make room in your heart for your friends and to look for opportunities to invite a friend into your life. I love the character L.M. Montgomery created in *Anne of Green Gables*. Anne Shirley was a wonderfully imaginative girl who, although she was an orphan,

> ❧❧
>
> "A BOSOM FRIEND — AN INTIMATE FRIEND, YOU KNOW, A REALLY KINDRED SPIRIT TO WHOM I CAN CONFIDE MY INMOST SOUL. I'VE DREAMED OF MEETING HER ALL MY LIFE. I NEVER REALLY SUPPOSED I WOULD, BUT SO MANY OF MY LOVELIEST DREAMS HAVE COME TRUE ALL AT ONCE THAT PERHAPS THIS ONE WILL, TOO. DO YOU THINK IT'S POSSIBLE?"
>
> *Anne of Green Gables*
>
> ❧❧

believed for the best and opened her heart to friendships with even the most unlikely people. She was always keen to find a "kindred spirit." When Anne is invited to stay at the home of her best friend Diana Barry, the two girls race around the house and jump on the bed of a spare guest bedroom, where they discover Diana's Aunt Josephine sleeping. Aunt Josephine is an old woman who Diana doesn't think was "ever a little girl." She is prim and proper and certain to scold the two girls for their unwelcome disruption into her night's rest. But when Anne comes back the next morning to apologize to Aunt Josephine, the old woman is soon disarmed by Anne's amusingly frank and open nature. Anne then remarks, "… you seem like an interesting lady, and you might even be a kindred spirit although you don't look very much like it."[25] She and Anne later become good friends. Anne Shirley learned that sometimes you can find friendships in the most unlikely people if you look hard enough and open your heart to them.

There are many ways to prioritize friendship and you can order your life in such a way that you create opportunities to invite people into your heart. Having a meal together is a wonderful way to get to cultivate friendship. In the early church, breaking bread together was a sign of unity and fellowship. It is still true today. When we invite someone over to share a meal, we invite them to share in our lives. When someone walks through your front door and sits down at your table to share a meal, she quickly goes from being mere acquaintance to someone who taken part in your everyday life. She is no longer a mere façade of a person, but a real flesh and blood friend who has seen your home, met your family and experienced life with you.

Getting a group of friends together for a fun event is another way to connect with friends, old and new. There is something about taking someone out of their usual context, whether it is work or church or school, and doing something enjoyable together that deepens the bonds of friendship. Try to plan a "ladies night out" every once in awhile. It is sometimes challenging, especially when it comes to coordinating several schedules and child care, but when it does happen, it can be so much fun. Women tend to open up to one another more readily when they are together, *sans* husbands.

But you can also include time with children and husbands. I have had some great conversations with other moms while we watch our kids are on the playground. It doesn't have to be overly frequent, but women are recharged and renewed by meaningful connection with other women, so it is important to plan it into your schedule.

You can also work friendship into your existing list of things to do. We are all busy, and there are some things that simply have to get done. Why not ask a friend to join you? Instead of getting your hair cut at the salon alone, you can easily invite another woman along and get simultaneous appointments. If you have a little extra time, you could both sneak in a manicure. You will get a little time to talk and you both feel pampered at the end. Best of all, you really haven't spent more time than you would have had you gone alone, and you have included a friend. You can also meet a friend while running errands. My sister lives nearby and we sometimes plan to meet at the grocery store. We both have to get food, and we can do a little talking while walking down the aisles. At least we feel like we have connected if only briefly. There are so many ways to make room for friendship if you think creatively and give friendship a place in your schedule. You will find that it is possible to order your life in such a way to open your heart to friends, both old and new. How much richer your life will be for it!

BE KIND TO YOUR FRIENDS

Henrietta Mears, a prominent Bible teacher and founder of Gospel Light Publications, was known to walk spiritually tall and elegantly, like a beautiful, gracious queen. She carried herself in a manner fitting for a King's daughter. When she walked into a room, people would sense her presence immediately. But when she entered a room, it was not with an attitude of "Here I am, the one you've been waiting for," but "There you are! I've been looking for you. How wonderful to see you."[26] She was enthusiastic about others.

A gracious woman doesn't focus on herself, but on other people. She expresses kindness and genuine concern for other people. She is not interested in making other people like her, but is trying to love others. Gracious women are enthusiastic about others and show this by being good listeners.

The world needs more listeners, and listening is an essential skill for a gracious woman. It is a skill that we can learn to do and become proficient in as we practice it. Being a good listener communicates kindness and caring to others. When we stop to focus our attention on what someone else is saying, we show them that we value them as people and that we care about what they have to share. When we are too busy talking about ourselves and never stop to give others our attention, we communicate to them that we are really not concerned about them but rather just want someone to listen to us. We may not realize it, but looking away when someone else is speaking, fidgeting or cutting someone off mid-sentence is sending a message that we don't care.

> *Listen* is such a little, ordinary word. Yet we all know the pain of not being listened to, of not being heard.... In a way, not to be heard is not to exist.[27]

As we become good listeners, we will show genuine kindness to others. Most people recognize a good listener immediately and are drawn to them. We all like to be around people that make us feel heard and validated. Even if you are the kind of woman who finds it easier to talk than to listen, you can learn to become more conscientious about listening and develop the skills necessary to being a good listener. Here are a few things to keep in mind.

1.   **Practice good eye contact.** Look at the person who is talking. This is probably the most telling sign that you are truly listening to what is being said.

2.   **Concentrate on what is being said, not on what you will say next.** Don't think about what your response will be until after you have heard everything that is said. Try to stay in the present moment and listen with your heart. Even wanting to appear like a good listener can be a distraction to true listening.

> Desires other than love get in the way of soul care dialogue. Even such benign desires as the wish to be helpful or to be experienced as a

good listener tend to be distractions from genuine dialogue as they encourage me to focus on myself. Only love leaves me free to set myself, including my needs and desires, to the side. Only love allows me to temporarily stand apart from my own experiences and construals of the world and enter deeply into those of the one for whom I seek to care.[28]

3.   ***Clarify and validate.*** Clarify what the other person is saying by repeating what you think they are saying in your own words. When you restate to someone what they have said, they feel they have been heard and their feelings validated.

4.   ***Let people finish their sentence before jumping in.*** Do not interrupt someone while she is speaking. You can agree and express your understanding with short phrases, but allow the person to complete their sentence and thought before offering your response.

5.   ***Ask questions.*** People love to talk about themselves, and even the quietest ones can be coaxed out of her shell by thoughtful questions. Initiate

conversations by asking others about themselves. It is a true sign that you care. Likewise, those who never ask any questions about others communicate that they don't genuinely care about people.

As you begin to develop the habits of good listening, you will be providing one of the greatest kindnesses you can to your friends. Gracious friends are those who listen with their hearts and genuinely connect with those they care for.

SHARE BEAUTY WITH OTHERS

Women love beautiful things and are inspired by beauty. As gracious women, we already have an eye for beauty, but we sometimes don't think of sharing that with others. One of the nicest things you can do for someone is to share something beautiful with them. Beauty inspires the soul, and when shared, that inspiration is doubled! There are many ways to share beauty with a friend.

Proverbs 18:16 tells us that "A gift opens the way for the giver and ushers him into the presence of the great." Give a gift of beauty to someone and you will not only brighten their day, but you will find an open door for a deeper friendship. Gifts don't have to be anything large or expensive, but a special hand-picked gift can say so much to someone.

Keep your eyes out for things that your friends like. I went through a period when I was keen on collecting pink Depression era glass, but I did not live near many antiques stores and the only way I could find them was online. One of my friends lived in a part of town that was filled with antique stores and she was always making treasure hunting trips. She would pick up little items for me and it always brightened my day. It wasn't only that I had a new piece to add to my collection, but that she had the heart to think of me during her shopping trips. I have learned from her to do the same.

> There are so many wonderful ways to share and express our warm feelings toward others. Do it as a natural part of your life, of your day. When you do things for yourself, include others in them. The next time you roast walnuts, roast some extra ones and wrap them to give to a friend you're meeting for lunch

tomorrow. When you discover a wine you particularly enjoy, buy an extra bottle, tie it with a ribbon and bring it to a friend. Drop a few museum postcards off at a friend's apartment house on your way home from work with a note, "Thinking of you." After you've been to a special museum exhibit, take the catalogue to an elderly friend who is confined to her home.[29]

When you share things with your friends, whether it is a gift or a letter, take a little extra effort to make it beautiful. You can easily make something very ordinary into something very beautiful by adding some embellishment in how you present your gift. A bar of chocolate from the grocery store becomes a present when you tuck it into a pretty bag lined with tissue paper and a bow. My sister in law Jenny always wraps her gifts in the most creative packages and loves including beautiful cards. It seems like a waste of money when she could easily just wrap them plainly. But an artfully wrapped present is a gift unto itself. Sometimes it doesn't matter what could be inside – the outside presentation was enough eye candy to be the present itself!

Consider designing or making or your stationery or greeting cards. A few intentional doodles can go a long ways in showing your friends an extra-amount of care. They don't have to look professional (that's the point!) or sound particularly poetic, but you could draw a little, paste on some pretty cut-outs, and copy a line of Scripture or poetry from something you have read. And don't forget to do something pretty with the envelope. Perhaps you could decorate it with some stickers. Or in the least, you could use some color in your address, but just make sure it is legible for the postal carrier!

You can also share beauty in so many other ways. Attend a museum exhibit with a friend. Marvel over the beautiful paintings and the talent it took to produce them. Visit a botanical garden with a friend. Make sure to bring your camera. There is nothing so wonderful as flowers in bloom. Take turns taking pictures of each other against the backdrop of colors! Go to a local antique fair and try to see who can find the best treasure. Invite some friends over for a movie night. Pick a costume drama and gush over the beautiful dresses. If you are having an overnight guest, add some fresh flowers to her room. Include an individual teapot and teabag and some pretty decorating books for her to browse through during her stay. Invite a friend over for afternoon tea, and spread out your fine linen and silverware. Some women have "dress up" tea parties where all the women come wearing hats and gloves!

Women love creating beauty too. I have been part of Bible study groups where the women periodically got together to do arts and crafts. One woman would teach us how do a project, and we all loved it because we got to do something creative together and at the end we all got to take home a thing of beauty! Some women love making jewelry and organize bracelet making parties where everyone can choose their own beads and baubles. Others love to scrapbook and can arrange scrapbooking events where women can create their own photo memory pages. Flower arranging, decoupage, painting pottery, and cross-stitching are all artistic projects that can be done with friends.

Whatever you do, there are so many ways to add beauty into your friendships. From gifts, to hosting a beautiful gathering, to sharing a creative activity, you will find your own soul refreshed as you share something beautiful with others.

FRIENDS FOREVER

Some friends come in and out of our lives and we are happy for the time that we have spent with them and the shared memories we keep, but there are other friends that we stand the test of time, separation and differences. I have one friend whom I met in the sixth grade and have remained friends with through the years. In the last twenty years, we have never lived in the same state, but our friendship has lasted through time, distance and even vast differences in lifestyle. She is a successful physician who lives in New York City and has never married. I am a suburban stay-at-home mom who spends most of her day chasing around my children.

The main reason we have remained close is not because we have a lot in common on the outside, but because we share the greatest life passion on the inside: a living faith in Jesus Christ. We share a bond in the Lord, and although we talk about all sorts of topics ranging from our families and hobbies, we know that our friendship is held together by our commitment to pray for one another and encourage each other in our Christian faith. I know that when I ask for to pray for me, she is faithful in bringing my requests before the Lord. We are also accountable to each other in how we live our lives. I know that she cares about my walk with God and I can trust her to encourage and even correct me when I falter. In the same way, she knows that I pray for her and that my desire for her is to see her growing in her relationship with God.

We all need friends who can lift us up when we are weak and pray for us when we can no longer pray. God gives us friends to encourage us and help us through life's trials. The presence of a friend can sustain us when we are tempted to give up. When we find a friend who is truly a kindred spirit in the Lord, we know that we have made a friend for life. More than that, we have made a friend for eternity. I think one of the most wonderful things about heaven will be that we will be reunited with old friends. Sometimes I think about what that will be like. We will praise the Lord together and continue our friendships on earth. Only, it will be even richer, because in heaven we will be freed from all our earthly hindrances to genuine friendship: the "masks" we wear, our selfishness, our pride. In heaven, we will experience the depths of true friendship that will continue for all of eternity. I am glad that we get a little taste of it on earth too. So make order your life to make some room for friendship. And remember to be kind to your friends. Finally, bring some beauty into another person's life. You will find it returned to you!

REFLECT AND RESPOND

1. Make a list of traits that you look for in a good friend. How can you be that sort of friend to someone else?

2. Plan a "girls day out" with some friends. Take time to re-connect and have some fun!

3. Mark down your friends' birthdays on a calendar. Acknowledge their special occasion with a card or gift.

4. Think of three friends, old or new, and keep them in your prayers this week. Be specific as you ask God to bless them.

5. Memorize Proverbs 17:17 "A friend loves at all times…"

THE GRACIOUS WOMAN AND HER WORLD

Chapter Seven

TENDER OF THE HEARTH:
The Gracious Woman and Her Home

"The wise woman builds her house…"
(Proverbs 14:1)

CREATING A GRACIOUS HOMELIFE

Life at home should be full of graciousness. Our homes should provide us with comfort and be safe havens from the busyness and storms of the world outside. They should also be places of beauty and creativity. They should be nests for our families to enjoy company, recreation, and laughter. Our homes are designed to be quiet places for us to experience God, pray, and study. They should welcome us home each night and send us off each morning to face another day. Our homes should also extend beyond our individual families to welcome friends with warmth and hospitality.

> The very heart of home is intimacy. For this is where we are the most ourselves. And when we have that inner calm, that is when we give the best parts of ourselves. A chair in a sunny corner where a child can learn to read, and later, perhaps, tell a secret or discuss a problem – that is the essence of what [home] is about… In the midst of today's hectic living, there still can exist in our homes a haven where we can savor the simple and charming things in life. [We can] celebrate the everyday eloquence of domestic rituals. From bathing and dressing in the morning to falling into slumber in the evening, these intimate spaces evoke a graceful world, one with time set aside for leisure and gentility… Here one can seek momentary sanctuary from the rigors of the day, relax and read or merely let the mind wander. Here one may be inspired to write or to paint, or perhaps to excel at the domestic arts. Here one can retire at the end of the day, to sleep the deep sleep of childhood and rise to greet the soft light of day through a veil of lace…[30]

The nucleus of a woman's world is her home.

All of her endeavors towards living graciously begin here. Women are instrumental in creating a culture of gracious living at home. Proverbs 14:1 tells us that the "wise woman builds her house" while the foolish one "tears hers down." The noble woman described in Proverbs 31 was one that watched over her household diligently. Women are tenders of the hearth. We keep the warm fire of a loving home aglow day and night. Whether we share an apartment with roommates or live in a stately mansion with a large family, we have the ability to foster an atmosphere of warmth and joy at home. As women, we are the emotional heart and barometer of the home. If we are gracious, we can spread light and warmth around a home. Our kindness and our joy for living make everyone else at home happier and more at peace. On the other hand, our bitterness and complaining can make all of the members of our home miserable!

The Victorians had a sense of a woman's ability to create a warm and beautiful homelife for her family. J.R. Miller, a turn of the century writer, commented:

Home is the true wife's kingdom. There, first
of all places, she must be strong and beautiful.
She may touch like outside in many ways, if she
can do it without slighting the duties that are
hers within her own doors. But if any calls for
her service must be declined, they should not
be the duties of her home. These are hers, and
no other one's. Very largely does the wife hold
in her hands, as a sacred trust, the happiness
and the highest good of the hearts that nestle
there. The best husband - the truest, noblest,
the gentlest, the richest-hearted - cannot make
his home happy if his wife be not, in every
reasonable sense, a help-mate to him. In the
last analysis, home happiness does depend on
the wife. Her spirit gives the home its
atmosphere. Her hands fashion its beauty. Her
heart makes its love. And the end is so worthy,
so noble, so divine, that no woman who has
been called to be a wife, and has listened to the
call, should consider any price too great to pay,
to be the light, the joy, the blessing, the
inspiration, of a home. Men with fine gifts
think it worth while to live to paint a few great
pictures which shall be looked at and admired
for generations; or to write a few songs which
shall sing themselves into the ears and hearts of
men. But the woman who makes a sweet,
beautiful home, filling it with love and prayer
and purity, is doing something better than
anything else her hands could find to do

beneath the skies.[31]

And so, we as women have the great joy and privilege of fostering an atmosphere of love and acceptance in our homes. I want my home to be a place that my children will always look back on with warm and happy memories. I want my husband to come home at the end of the day and feel at once that he can leave the burdens of his day outside and come home to peace and rest.

The first step in creating a gracious homelife is dedicating your family and home to God. Through God's indwelling Spirit, we can taste a little bit of heaven on earth through a happy home and the love of family. This sort of a home is not made by fancy things, but by the love we put into it. There is no substitute for good relationships between husbands and wives, parents and children. No amount of fancy furniture, fine window dressings, or paintings will make up for a lack of love in the house. Proverbs 15:17 and 17:1 remind us that it is better to have a "meal of vegetables where there is love than a fattened calf with hatred" and "dry crust with peace and quiet than a house full of feasting and strife." In other words, the most important thing about your home is allowing God to come and dwell in the heart of the home through each person who lives there.

Begin by making sure your priorities are

> "TO MAKE HOME HAPPY IS ONE OF THE CHIEF OFFICES OF WOMEN; AND IT IS THE CENTRE OF ALL THAT IS SWEET IN THE SYMPATHIES, AND DEAR IN THE AFFECTIONS OF THE SOUL, FOR THERE ALL SHOULD BE SINCERE, CORDIAL, AND CANDID."
>
> *Daisy Eyebright*

where they should be: in investing your time and love into the people who live at home. All of the other tasks around taking care of a home, arranging pretty furnishings, making home-cooked meals, organizing your routine, will follow. The most important thing is letting God's love permeate through the walls of your home.

With God's grace abiding in your home, you can then begin to put into practice the three main principles of gracious living as it concerns our homes. You can create and orderly home, one where things are put in their proper place and tasks are effectively prioritized. Your home can also be an extension of kindness as you use it in the art of hospitality. Finally, you can make your home a place where beauty surrounds each person who walks through your front door.

Keeping an Ordered Home

Did you know that God is orderly? When God created the universe he created something out of nothing and then brought order out of chaos by separating the light from the darkness, the water from the land. I Corinthians 14:3 tells us that God is not a God of disorder but of peace. So as we grow closer to the Lord and become more Christlike, we will find that He will bring order out of the chaos of our lives, and that includes order into our homes!

Keeping a clean, orderly home is important because it reflects a disciplined, ordered life. But it is not just a means in itself. When we keep to an ordered schedule and keep our homes neat and clean, we find that we have more time to do other things.

Initially, it may take some time to get our homes and schedules ordered, but once we do, we should find that we have more time in our day. When we designate a proper place for things, we will spend less time searching for objects around the house. When we learn how to handle out housekeeping tasks more efficiently, we find that chores which used to take us hours no longer consume so much of our time.

Sometimes we approach the daily tasks of keeping an orderly home as mundane and unimportant. We look at housekeeping in terms of dust bunnies and dish cloths. But housekeeping should really be viewed as homemaking. Making a home is a noble endeavor and even an art. The home is the fundamental unit of society and contributes significantly to how we feel about our lives as a whole. Samuel Johnson, an 18th century writer wrote, "To be happy at home is the ultimate result of all ambition, the end to which every enterprise and labor tends, and of which every desire prompts the prosecution." When you begin to realize how important making a home is, the little tasks that we do are infused with new meaning.

> Much of enjoying life is in the details- the
> larger issues have a way of working themselves
> out. Handling daily tasks well and thoroughly
> affects how we feel, our happiness and the
> overall quality of our lives.…. By creating
> beauty and order where you live and work you
> will be controlling the private hours of your
> life. Home, especially is one area of existence
> where you can have control. By concentrating
> on easy, positive steps- the kind of toothpaste
> and shampoo and body cream you use, the
> contour and color of your sheets, the firmness
> of your mattress, a sunny place set up for
> lunch, the temperature of your room and tub
> water- the smells and colors that surround you-
> these are the things that you can make right for
> yourself.[32]

To live graciously at home is to find purpose
and meaning in our daily "chores" and to do them
creatively and cheerfully. We can perform our home
duties with reverence for the beauty of the mundane,
elevating everyday tasks into a gentle art.[33] Taking
care of our home, whether it is cleaning, cooking or
organizing, can be done in such a way that we find
meaning and purpose in what we are doing. When
my first child was born, I became a full-time at-home

mom. At first, I didn't see my home duties as a "job" to work at with excellence or something to take pride in. After all, I thought, a job was something I did outside of the home. But I soon realized that my being at home full time meant that home was now truly my domain, and something that I should cultivate and tend to as diligently as I would a career. I began to realize that my role as a homekeeper was one of great significance and dignity. After all, I ensure the cleanliness of our home for my children and husband. I am responsible for providing healthy, tasty food that will help them grow physically and nourish their souls. I make sure everyone looks good (clothes washed, shirts ironed, hair combed!) I am entrusted with our family finances by shopping wisely. I

> ✍
>
> "LORD OF ALL POTS AND PANS AND THINGS... MAKE ME A SAINT BY GETTING MEALS AND WASHING UP THE PLATES.... THE TIME OF BUSINESS DOES NOT WITH ME DIFFER FROM THE TIME OF PRAYER AND IN THE NOISE AND CLATTER OF MY KITCHEN... I POSSESS GOD IN AS GREAT TRANQUILITY AS IF I WERE UPON MY KNEES AT THE BLESSED SACRAMENT."
>
> *Brother Lawrence*
>
> ✍

provide a beautiful, serene atmosphere in which my family can rest and recharge. What a great responsibility I have for taking care of my home! And so I began to find ways to order my home duties in such a way that I realize their full potential and significance.

> Creating daily rituals- making daily tasks into times of enrichment through planning and special personal details- is a way to live a richer, more satisfying life.... It takes a commitment to enjoy each day fully. And it takes respect for the significance of grace. "Rituals" is my term for patterns you create in your everyday living that uplift the way you do ordinary things, so that a simple task rises to the level of something special, ceremonial, ritualistic.[34]

There are a few main areas to think about in order to keep an ordered home. They are cleaning, organizing, preparing meals and managing your time. Below are a few suggestions for each of those areas.

1. *Clean and Organize Like a Pro.* Some people are neat and organized by nature, and for others, it is a major challenge keeping even one room of the house clean. Don't get overwhelmed if you fall

into the latter category. You don't have to tackle cleaning your entire house at once. Firstly, try to have a place for everything in your home. If you know where something belongs, it is much easier to keep your house organized. Keeping items in their proper place is a key to organizing your home. Invest in some durable bins, baskets, or boxes to store items which you do not use regularly. Mark what it inside each box and keep like-minded items together. Store seasonal items in labeled boxes. Keep items you use regularly in easy-to-find places. Get rid of unused items around the house. If you don't use all those plastic containers and glass jars that you have been storing in your cupboards, throw them out! Go through your closets and evaluate what clothes you really wear. Except for a few special occasion items, get rid of clothes which you haven't worn for over two years. I almost always keep a donation bag in my closet and when it is full, I bring it to Goodwill or the Salvation Army. If you purchase a new item of clothing, see if you can replace it with something you no longer wear. I also practice "cleaning as you go."

Sometimes it is hard to carve out large chunks of uninterrupted time to clean my house, so I try to pick up and tidy things as I see them. I keep cleaning supplies easily accessible. I store a roll of paper towels under each sink of my house, so that I never have an excuse not to wipe down a counter when I see the need. Little steps towards keeping things neat go a long way in keeping my entire house clean.

2.　　*Cook like a Chef.* Again, for some people, cooking comes easily and with great pleasure. For others, it is a challenge not burning a frozen pizza. I fall into the latter category. I am neither good at cooking nor do I particularly enjoy the process, but I really do want to provide meals that are healthy and appetizing for my family.

> If the one who cooks is the wife in a family, her attitude toward the marriage as a whole should be to think of it as a career. Being challenged by what a difference her cooking and her way of serving is going to make in the family life gives a woman an opportunity to approach this with a feeling of painting a picture or writing a symphony.[35]

So, what does a cooking disaster like me do? Firstly, I find it helpful to flip through cookbooks and look at the pictures. If you want your meals to be appetizing, you need to be excited about cooking them. Looking at the pictures in cookbooks waters my own appetite and gets me excited to cook. It also helps shake me out of my rut of 3-4 constant dishes. It has also helped me to make a list of meals that I am very comfortable making. When I started to write everything down, I discovered that I could actually make a lot more meals than I had thought I could. I once turned my "meal list" into a pretty paper menu and asked my husband to choose which dishes he wanted to have that week. I found that when I treated my kitchen like a restaurant, I started to have a more professional attitude towards cooking. Some families have menu chalkboards where meals are attractively highlighted each day. I have also found that it helps to watch others cook. Ask your friends for their favorite recipes, tune in to a cooking show every once in awhile, or check out your local community college for cooking classes. Try different methods of cooking. Crock pots are great, especially in the winter. Stir fry, bake, steam, stew… do a little of each to keep your meals varied and interesting. Finally, it is okay to have backup plans and exit strategies! I keep a few "dinners in a bag" in our freezer for quick meals and "emergency burns." These ideas are ways to bring structure and creativity to your cooking.

3. **_Manage your time well._** Not everyone likes using a day-planner, but everyone should have a method of scheduling appointments and organizing their days. I handwrite appointments into a calendar as well as schedule "pop-up" reminders on my computer to keep myself up to date. There are some things I just wouldn't remember if I didn't write them down. Sometimes on particularly hectic days, I make a "To Do" list so I won't forget anything. It helps me clarify and prioritize what needs to be done, and gives me a sense of accomplishment as I cross off tasks as they get done. On days that are extremely busy, I will often write down an hourly list. That way, I can keep

myself on schedule. I also try to include free "flex time" in my day to catch up on things or just take a break.

As I work through my daily and weekly tasks around the house, it is easy to lose sight of the meaning and purpose of housework. I often get bogged down somewhere between chasing down a renegade band of Cheerios underneath the couch and making sure I don't overcook the chicken (again!) It helps to remind myself of verses like Proverbs 14:1 and Proverbs 31:27 which describe an ideal woman who "watches over the affairs of her household and does not eat the bread of idleness." A woman's role in caring for her home is more than just the physical duties that make up housework. No indeed, excellence in the house is a reflection of her character, her inner strength and the legacy she provides for her family.

ENTERTAINING ANGELS UNAWARE

The second principle in gracious living is kindness. Did you know that you can extend kindness through your home? In fact, opening our homes to others is one of the *best* ways to express kindness because our homes express who we are at the core of our being. And opening the front door is a way of opening the door of our hearts. The Bible tells us that some people have even welcomed angels into their homes by simply putting out their welcome mats. "Do not forget to entertain strangers, for by so doing some people have entertained angels without knowing it" (Hebrews 13:2). Hospitality is an act of Christian kindness.

But sometimes, instead of offering our homes as outlets for sharing, we make them fortresses and personal kingdoms for ourselves. We forget that God blesses us with a home, *in order* for us to share it with others. He wants us to open the doors to friends, extended family, and even strangers. Ravi Zacharias in his book *Jesus Among Other Gods* tells the story of what began as one of the worst Christmases of his life. His family had been through a very difficult time and as the holiday season approached, their daughter had been taken to the hospital for the birth of her first child. On Christmas evening, the whole house was in disarray, and everyone was emotionally edgy. To make matters worse, his mother-in-law had invited a gentleman from their church to have dinner with them. No one knew this man very well except that he came to their church and always sat alone. He was an odd man who seemed to be without friends or family. So, while everyone else was in frantically rushing around the house, Ravi was left with the task of entertaining this man. At first Ravi was not happy that the time he had hoped to spend with his family was being given instead to this man who engaged him in what became a heavy theological discussion. But at the end of the night, the solitary man left their home and thanked the family for what he said was "the best Christmas of my whole life." Ravi reflected:

> My heart sank in self-indictment at those tender words of his. I had to draw on every nerve in my being to keep from breaking down with tears. Just a few short years later, relatively young, and therefore to our surprise, he passed away. I have relived that Christmas many times in my memory. The Lord taught me a lesson. The primary purpose of a home is to reflect and to distribute the love of Christ.

Anything that usurps that is idolatrous.[36]

So, how do we begin to make our homes a haven for guests? We begin by opening our hearts to people. Like many things in life, hospitality is something we can either *seem* to do or something we can genuinely *be*. Most magazine articles that talk about hospitality focus on the external details of decorating a guest room, setting a table properly, inviting friends for a party. These are all considerate and valuable, but true hospitality is more concerned with the warmth of our personalities and opening our hearts to allow other people into our personal spaces and lives. .

Opening our hearts to people means giving them our time. As Dorothy C. Bass observes in her book, *Receiving the Day*, "In an era when many of us feel that time is our scarcest resource, hospitality falters... 'In a fast-food culture,' a wise Benedictine monk observes, 'you have to remind yourself that some things cannot be done quickly. Hospitality takes time.'"[37] Sitting down with a friend over a cup of tea inevitably means carving out time in our busy schedules to give her our uninterrupted attention. We do this because we value people and care about sharing our lives, and that always means sharing our time.

Hospitality also means loving people more than things. I love to decorate my house with pretty things but I have never wanted my home to be a museum where people feel like they can't sit on the furniture. I want people to feel at home. When we have overnight guests, I want them to fee so comfortable that they can visit our kitchen in the middle of the night to make themselves a snack. I want them to treat our home like theirs.

Hospitality involves giving attention to the needs of others. When preparing to have friends over for dinner, we should be more concerned about making them feel comfortable and welcomed than impressing them with our flower arrangements or gourmet meals. Again, I love the two verses in Proverbs which remind us that, "a meal of vegetables where there is love is better than a fattened calf with hatred" and "a dry crust with peace and quiet is better than a house full of feasting, with strife."[38] Those two verses remind me to put sincerity and acceptance ahead of decorations and presentation.

Our homes can be used in many ways to serve the Lord. You can have Bible studies and fellowship meetings in your home. It is often easier to invite unsaved friends to attend a Bible study in someone's home than asking them to step foot into a church building on a Sunday morning. Homes are wonderfully warm atmospheres for groups to gather. We have opened our home to special youth group events as well as business functions. In the summer, we like to throw some hot dogs and burgers on the grill and host an outdoor party. Some people have book clubs where they invite their neighbors and friends to gather for tea and stimulating conversation. You could host a neighborhood play group in your house. There are so many opportunities to use your home as a blessing to others.

We have also had overnight visitors and extended guests in our home, from relatives to friends in need. If you have a dedicated room in your house for guests, make sure it is both functional and a little special. Spend an evening in your own guest room. This is the best way to make sure the room is practical for a visitor. Is there enough lighting in the room? Are the blankets warm enough? Is the alarm clock at a reachable distance and set at a comfortable volume? Would your guests like a carafe or basket of snacks in the room?

There are many ways in which we can let God use our homes to bless others. And as we open our doors to others, we will find that our home lives will not diminish, but instead become even more rich.

A PLACE TO CELEBRATE BEAUTY

Your home is a place that reflects you and your family members' unique personalities and the memories you share. I love going to someone's home for the first time. I can usually sense something about their personality just as I step inside and I always come away feeling like I have gotten a glimpse of the real person inside. You can perceive individuality by looking at what people have put up on their walls, which sorts of books line their shelves, what special objects they have chosen to display. Our homes are our most personal space, our own very own little world that we have created to express our likes and values.

A home is a place where beauty is celebrated. I think that there is something about surrounding oneself with beautiful things. Please note that I didn't mean to say *expensive* things, but *beautiful* things, because beautiful objects and decorations do not have to cost a lot of money. Beauty can be found in very simple things. Cuttings from your garden, a spray of fallen fall leaves, amateur watercolors… all of these very inexpensive things can be things of beauty if we have an eye to appreciate them and place them in spots around the house where they enhance decor. Cherished photographs, precious souvenirs from memorable vacations, special gifts from love ones… all of these objects have meaning and value beyond their material worth and bring beauty into a space.

Each person has an individual style and taste. If you are searching to define your individual style, it may be helpful to look through decorating magazines or catalogs and clip out things that you like. I have binders full of clippings I have collected over the years from *Victoria* Magazine and *Romantic Homes*. Once you have a sense of what your general style is, you can begin decorating or re-decorating your home.

Creating a beautiful home is a blessing for the whole family. There is something about being in beautiful surroundings that makes life just a little bit sweeter. A pitcher of ice water or lemonade in the summer recalls a gentler age when poured from a pretty glass pitcher into glasses decorated with lemon slices and mint sprigs. Think of the intangible extra something that a vase of fresh flowers makes in a room. A beautiful office makes work more productive. An elegant bedroom seems to make sleep more restful. Beauty even in a bathroom seems to make a woman feel more beautiful herself. Even children can sense beauty in a home.

> Children growing up in an atmosphere where beauty is considered an important part of daily life cannot help being inspired to develop their original ideas in these areas, nor can they help begin prepared to live aesthetically themselves.

…Instead of saying, "Oh it doesn't matter, it's only the children", when you are along with children for a meal, it is important to say the opposite to yourself. "I wonder what the children would enjoy the most? Being surprised by something special on the table – a mirror with a new toy duck on it, and some stones around the edge so that it looks like a pond, lighted by candles in crystal candlesticks, or pewter candlesticks… something that will look like lamps near the pond? Or would they rather have a choice, since they are the ones to be considered tonight… shall we have the green cloth, or the pink with pink candles?" It can be something that takes very little time indeed… Imagination not only provides a background of beauty to daily life, but also a realization that love, thought and preparation has been given to that "together" time of eating.[39]

Make your home beautiful. Opt for pretty things if you have the choice. Even useful items can be pretty. Kitchen utensils and storage containers can be both practical and beautiful to look at. Choose beauty whenever you can! A wicker basket to hold extra hand towels, painted glass tumblers, a set of attractive canisters for the kitchen are all nicer than their plain counterparts.

And don't forget the beauty of good food either! Preparing meals can be an expression of beauty and creativity. Besides providing for your family's physical health, meals offer a central gathering point for building relationships and cultivating family bonds. Everyone loves to enjoy the taste of good food, especially when shared with others. Like the term "comfort food" suggests, food can have effects that reach far beyond the stomach. There is an emotional component in food. God has given us flavor and taste as a gift to be enjoyed.

> Food should be chosen for nutritive values, of course, but also to give variety and interest to meals. Food should be chosen to give pleasure, and to cheer up people after a hard day's work, to comfort them when they feel down for some reason, to amuse them when things seem a bit dull, or to open up conversation when they feel silent and uncommunicative…. Perhaps part of the reason why some people dislike cooking or find meal preparation a bore, is that they get into a rut where menus are concerned. Variety makes food more interesting to cook, as well as to serve and eat.[40]

Making meals appetizing and interesting, as well as presenting them beautifully does not necessarily mean that much extra work either. It only requires a little forethought and preparation. Sit down at the beginning of the week and think through your menu. Don't be afraid to try new recipes. "Variety is the spice of life," the old saying goes. A little variety goes a long way, especially for those of us who aren't naturally creative with food.

> A variety of taste treats is the spice of life. We all can become deadened to taste if we don't have surprise flavors in our everyday food to add some zip. After you've read some cookbooks and learned the basic principles of cooking, there should be a certain amount of serendipity. Experiment with your basic menus. Add ginger and blanched scallions and Greek olives to your chicken one night; the next, nutmeg, bacon and sour cream to your spinach. Then add a touch of soy sauce to whatever you have in the wok.[41]

And don't forget the presentation. Two little votive candles on the table can make all the difference in the world. A special pitcher can transform a meal. Try adding simple garnishes: a sliced lemon to squeeze over seafood, sprigs of fresh herbs over chicken. Have you ever been to a fine restaurant when they "paint a plate" by drizzling sauce over the dish with artistic flair? You could try that with many dishes that you probably already make. You can also do wonders in food presentation just by varying your dishware. Try using different plates or unusual containers for food. Different colors enhance the look of food. Sushi on a square black plate looks more exotic. For more formal occasions, don't forget floral arrangements, interesting place cards, folded napkins and silverware settings.

HEART OF THE HOME

Fashioning a gracious home life is at the heart of gracious living. As a gracious woman, you have the power to transform four walls into a warm, loving, beautiful space for you and your family and friends. It is in the details of what we do and the love with which our hands work at each meaningful task. One of my favorite articles about homemaking comes from an issue of *Victoria* magazine. It is called "Special Touches of Beauty".

Those who make the extra effort may sometimes wonder if it's worthwhile, especially on a day when no one seems to notice that the bread is freshly made, even though the house is full of the scent of its rising. But then, she has only to search her heart and remember what she cherishes of her own childhood, the territory where the memories lie: the way the crystal pitcher made a rainbow of the light when the table was set, perhaps, the starched curtains that blew in the window, or the cinnamon toast Mother cut into butterflies. These are the epiphanies that lie beneath the surface of the rush through life at home, the "grace of the quotidian" as author Susannah Lessard puts it — grace unsought, and caught forever, a landscape of unassuming beauty where a woman's touch has smoothed the way.[42]

Never forget the importance of the love and care you put into your home. Keeping an ordered house, showing kindness through hospitality, and creating a beautiful space for those who live in it will be cherished for years to come.

REFLECT AND RESPOND

1. Read Proverbs 31:10-31. What was this woman's attitude towards her home?

2. Make a list for yourself of weekly household duties. Put it on a schedule for yourself. What are some other ways you can organize your household?

3. Add something fresh to your house this week. It can be fresh flowers, a centerpiece of colorful fruit, or even some fall leaves gathered from your yard.

4. Memorize Proverbs 14:1 "The wise woman builds her house, but with her own hands the foolish one tears hers down."

Chapter Eight

CHASER OF DREAMS:
The Gracious Woman and Her Career

"Let her works bring her praise at the city gate."
(Proverbs 31:31)

CELEBRATING VOCATION

Women come in all shapes and sizes. Some women are married while others remain single. Some women have children while others do not. But most women, at some point in their lives, will work at some sort of job. Most of the single women that I know work full time. Many married women work before they have children, and some moms continue working from home, or part-time outside of the home, even after they have children. Many stay-at-home moms eventually go back to work after their children are grown.

The Bible also gives us examples of women that worked. Although we usually think of the Proverbs 31 woman as the consummate wife and homemaker, the Bible tells us that she was also a successful businesswoman. She was diligent in helping to provide for her family by selling and trading. Lydia, a single woman noted in the book of Acts, was a merchant. Priscilla worked alongside her husband in his tent-making business. And Debra was an Old Testament judge whose counsel was sought by the Israelites.

The truth is, whether women are homemakers or teachers or doctors or lawyers, all women are working. Work is a necessary part of our humanity. When God created Adam and Eve, He gave them the job of cultivating the earth and being fruitful in it. He did not create them just so that they could live happy, listless lives, but so that they could make an impact on the earth and be examples of His productivity in creation. Working in a meaningful way is also essential to our self-esteem and mental health.

But for many of us, whether we work in the home or outside of the home, we view work as a necessary evil that we must contend with

> **"THE GLORY OF GOD IS A HUMAN BEING FULLY ALIVE."**
>
> *St. Irenaeus*

through most of our lives. Women who work at home and those who work outside of the home both feel the strain and burden of their jobs. Many women today must work to support themselves and sometimes even their families. Sometimes their work keeps them so busy that they are physically exhausted and feel pulled in many directions. Other women feel discouraged because they feel like their jobs are meaningless or boring, and they can not seem to achieve the success and recognition they desire.

God created men and women to be involved in *meaningful* work. But most of us work mainly because we need to earn a living. Our primary reason for going to the office every morning is not to fulfill God's calling on our lives but to earn enough money to pay the bills and provide for our physical needs. The focus is temporal, on what we need to do to get by in this life.

To work at a job only to provide for temporal needs is bound to produce a life lacking both direction and energy. On the other hand, people who have found their calling in life are full of purpose and overflowing with enthusiasm. They work hard, but their hard work almost seems like play to them. They have a sense of fulfillment and purpose when they are doing what they were created for. In addition, they are usually successful doing what they are called to do.

God's idea of work was not meant to be endless toil with benefits for only this life, but of a vocation, or calling, which has implications for eternity. The word *vocation* comes from the Latin word *vocare* which means "to call." The idea is that of an invitation, a special appointment, a destiny that God specifically has for you to fulfill. Because this life is a preparation for eternity, how we spend all of the resources God has given us, including our time and talents, should have some value in eternity. We should view our jobs in this light too.

As a gracious woman, you are called to celebrate and enjoy your vocation. Your job should be meaningful and bring you joy. In fact, I would venture to say that your job can be a means of fulfilling your dreams. God gives us dreams in our hearts and He wants us to trust Him to turn them into reality. We are to be dream chasers!

A gracious woman orders her life around discovering what God has called her to do. She makes it a priority to arrange her work around her vocation and God's will for her. Secondly, a gracious woman finds ways to bring kindness to those she works with. There are so many opportunities to be kind to others at work. If you work with non-Christians, your kindness may be the glimpse of Jesus that they desperately need to see. And finally, a gracious woman creates beauty through her work. A gracious heart produces a life of beauty, and beauty can infiltrate even the workplace.

Discovering God's Will

Frederick Buechner, in his book *Listening to Your Life,* provides a good summary of what a vocation is. He calls it the "kind of work God calls you to."

> The kind of work God usually calls you to is the kind of work (a) that you need most to do and (b) that the world most needs to have done. If you really get a kick out of your work, you've presumably met requirement (a), but if your work is writing TV deodorant commercials, the chances are you've missed requirement (b). On the other hand, if your work is being a doctor in a leper colony, you have probably met requirement (b), but if most of the time you're bored and depressed by it, the chances are you have not only bypassed (a) but probably aren't helping your patients much either. Neither the hair shirt nor the soft berth will do. The place God calls you to is the place where your deep gladness and the world's deep hunger meet.[43]

So how do we go about discovering God's will for us and ordering our lives around His calling, or our vocation? Firstly, let us consider what a vocation is so that we can understand what it means to us personally.

1. ***A vocation is something to which you are called.*** There is a sense of destiny, an excitement for the future and a knowing that you are chosen for this special task. It is often something that colors your entire life. A vocation is not something that you turn on at 9:00 in the morning and clock out of at 5:00 in the evening. It is something that involves your entire personality, your life's mission, your dreams.

2. ***A vocation utilizes the spiritual gifts, talents, skills and personality traits that God has given you.*** Whether a vocation is something designed especially for you or whether you have been created for such a vocation, it is something that you will find a natural competence for. Your gifts, skills and personality (how you are "wired") all work together to fit you for your special calling. Even your life experiences, both your successes and failures, will

have produced in you the unique ability to fulfill your calling.

3.	*A vocation should make a significant impact on the world, whether that means five people or five million people.* God calls us to leave the world a better place than we had found it. In fact, your life mission as a Christian should in some way be a continuation of Jesus' life mission. He came to save and heal and restore people to God and to one another. You may not impact thousands of people, but as your life intersects with one or two, He wants you to be a blessing that will impact them for eternity. This work does not always mean full-time ministry in the traditional sense of the word. We are called to be in ministry whether we are on the mission field in a third world country or in an office building where the mission field is dressed in suits and ties.

4.   ***A vocation will bring joy.*** You will have a sense of fulfillment that only living in your purpose can give you. You should enjoy your work and love what you do. The movie *Chariots of Fire* told the true story of Eric Liddell, an Olympic runner who was also called to the mission field in China. But for a time, he was also called to be a runner. "I believe God made me for a purpose," Liddell said, "for China. But He also made me fast. And when I run, I feel His pleasure." Although Liddell later went to China and died a martyr there, he first became a witness on the world stage as a committed Christian who honored God before personal success. His work, whether it was overtly spiritual, as it was in China, or seemingly secular, as it was on the track, brought him joy.

Those are some characteristics of what a vocation is. God has called you to something very special and tailored just for you, but how to do you go about finding what that something is? Begin by learning to hear God's voice and follow His leading. God answers prayer and will often speak to us while we are on our knees. Come to God as honestly as you can, and resolve to be open to obeying what He tells you. We may not have the strength on our own to obey, but if our hearts desire to be open, God will help us. The idea that God would speak to us in this day and age might seem to you like an episode of *Twilight Zone*. But the truth is that God does indeed speak into our lives. It may not come by way of a thunderbolt, but He does speak in many ways: firstly, through His Word (the Bible). Secondly He sometimes speaks to us through opportunities, other people, and His still, small voice that we hear in our souls. As we pray and give our personal dreams to God, He will begin to reveal His dream for our lives, which always turns out to be bigger and better than what we had hoped for on our own. The key is to pray, ask God for wisdom, search His Word for understanding and be open to hearing Him speak in whatever way He chooses.

Sometimes God's will may be a complete 180 degree U-turn from the path you had been on. He may call you to take a risk and step out in faith to fulfill your dream of starting a business. God may give you a vision for another people group and call you halfway across the globe. He may open up an opportunity for you to work in a completely different job that you didn't know existed. God may call you to leave your job and stay home instead.

In other cases, hearing God's voice may not lead to drastic change but will bring a deeper understanding of the life that you are *already* leading, and perhaps the work that you are already doing. As you seek the Lord for His will, you may discover that your heart has been His all along and He has already been leading you in the seemingly ordinary circumstances of your life, to bring you straight into the purposes He has for you. And with this deeper understanding of your calling, you will find new life and energy as you realize how significant your life and work really is.

> [He] learned to accept God's will "not as we might wish it, or as we thought in our poor human wisdom it ought to be," but rather as "the twenty-four hours of each day: the people, the places, the circumstances set before us in that time." He realized he had always approached life with an expectation of what God's will should be, and assumed God would help him fulfill that. Instead, he had to accept as God's will the actual circumstances faced each day, most of which lay outside of his control. [He wrote,] "Each day to me should be more than an obstacle to be gotten over, a span of time to be endured, a sequence of hours to be survived. For me, each day came forth from the hand of God newly created and alive with opportunities to do His will.... We for our part can accept and offer back to God every prayer, work, and suffering of the day, no matter how insignificant or unspectacular they may seem to us... Between God and the individual soul, however, there are no insignificant moments; this is the mystery of divine providence."[44]

Often, finding our life's purpose is more about doing less than doing more. In many cases, we are already doing something related to our vocation, or the calling that God has on our lives, but we are distracted by a multitude of other demands and tasks. We are busy and active, but we have accomplished little. When we focus on the purpose that God has called us to, we will find that we are more effective that we could have ever imagined. When light is diffuse, it is hazy and not even good enough for someone to read by it. But when light is concentrated to a single point, it becomes a laser so powerful that it can cut through the strongest of materials.

> There is nothing quite as potent as a focused life, one lived on purpose. The men and women who have made the greatest difference in history were the most focused. If you want your life to have impact, focus it! Stop dabbling. Stop trying to do it all. Prune away even good activities and do only that which matters most. Never confuse activity with productivity. You can be busy without a purpose, but what's the point? Paul said, "Let's keep focused on that goal, those of us who want everything God has for us."[45]

Discover what God's will is for your life and order your life around living in your vocation. That is where you will find the greatest meaning and significance for your work, whatever that work is.

OPPORTUNITIES FOR KINDNESS

Your job is a minefield of opportunities to show true kindness to others, because your job connects you with people. Whether it is to your co-workers, people that come into your job from the outside, or even your boss, there are many relationships which can be touched by kindness.

The office is often a place of great activity, deadlines and tasks. But for a Christian woman, the office is also a mission field and a place where you can reach out to non-believers and fellow believers alike. It will change the way you see your job if you view your workplace in this light, as a place brimming with potential friendships and opportunities to be a witness for the Lord. You may be the only "Bible" some of your coworkers will ever read, and the Lord may have placed you at your office to be an example of what a joyful, vibrant Christian is like. Begin to recognize the people that God has placed in our lives and how significant you may be in their journey to accepting Christ. The funny thing is that these people and our opportunities to bless them often come in the form of "interruptions" to our carefully orchestrated schedules.

> There is a popular epigram, generally attributed to John Lennon, which claims that "life is what happens to you while you're busy making other plans." In a similar vein, the Christian apologist C.S. Lewis asserts that what we call interruptions are precisely our real lives, the lives God sends us daily... the "interruptions" are the people who come to us in need of our service. They, like the people who comprise our families and our circles of friends, are what – or who – happen to us. Our relations and interactions with them form the sum and substance of our lives, giving content and form and meaning to our life stories.[46]

Whatever work we do, God wants us to be aware of the people that He has put around us. Sometimes it is hard to see their needs when we are faced with a pressing deadline, but if we allow the Holy Spirit to soften our hearts and open our eyes, we will begin to become sensitive to a hurting soul or a lonely heart.

Eugene Peterson, in his book *A Long Obedience*

---

in the Same Direction describes how God wants us to view our work. We are to view people as the primary reason and purpose for wherever we work and whatever we are doing there.

> For it makes very little difference how much money Christians carry in their wallets or purses. It makes little difference how our culture values and regards our work… unless. For our work creates neither life nor righteousness. Relentless, compulsive work habits ("the bread of anxious toil") which our society rewards and admires are seen by the psalmist as a sign of weak faith and assertive pride, as if God could not be trusted to accomplish His will, as if we could rearrange the universe by our own effort. What does make a difference is the personal relationships that we create and develop. We learn a name; we start a friendship; we follow up on a smile – or maybe even on a grimace. Nature is profligate with its seeds, scattering them everywhere; a few of them sprout. Out of numerous handshakes and greetings, some germinate and grow into a friendship in Christ. Christian worship gathers the energy and focuses the motivation which transforms us from consumers who work to get things into people who are intimate and in whom work is a way of being in creative relationship with another. Such work can be done within the structure of any job, career or profession. As

Christians do the jobs and tasks assigned to them in what the world calls work, we learn to pay attention to and practice what God is doing in love and justice, in helping and healing, in liberating and cheering.[47]

Some women are very good at making their workplaces a place where friendships bloom, and there are creative ways that you can encourage friendship, even in a busy corporate office. You can make a pretty "sharing basket" or box for your coworkers. Include such essentials as hand cream, needle and thread, safety pins, tea bags, wrapped candy and packets of microwave popcorn. Be creative and invite those who work with you to contribute their own "community items."

I knew one secretary who started a community candy jar. She bought bags of candy and kept an "open door policy" for anyone to come and help themselves. She also placed a bowl next to it with a small sign that read "Please chip in if you can. I buy the candy with my own money." Her co-workers regularly contributed change or a dollar when they could, and she was able to keep the candy supply flowing without spending a fortune out of her own funds!

Most of all, be available and open to developing genuine friendships with those people you work with. Some of them might seem completely different from your usual circle of friends, especially from your Christian friends. But they are people whom God loves and perhaps He has placed you in their lives for such a time as this so that your kindness will help open their hearts to Him.

MAKE YOUR WORK BEAUTIFUL

Some jobs create beauty by nature. I think of women who run wonderful boutiques, artists who create handmade works of beauty, and gardeners who nurture little seedlings into colorful blooms of beauty. Some women are called to work in professions that produce beautiful things and spread beauty to others. But even those whose jobs seemingly have very little to do with beauty can find ways to create something beautiful through their work. The key is to look for beauty and ways to bring it out in what you do.

Firstly, make sure the place where you work is beautiful. You want to feel inspired and welcomed in when you walk into your office. Keep fresh flowers and pretty artwork around. Bring in things from home. Include framed pictures of your loved ones and display special cards that you have received. Borrow a lamp from your house if your space needs more light.

Another way to create beauty is to make your work beautiful, whatever it is that you do, by doing your work with excellence. Martin Luther said, "A dairy maid can milk cows to the glory of God." Whether your job is waiting tables, teaching children, or drawing up important contracts, you can do your job to the very best of your ability. Sloppy work reflects poorly on you and can even be a hindrance to your Christian witness in the workplace. So, be sure to check your work before presenting it to others. Make sure you present the very best that you can do. If your job involves typing documents, a simple spelling and grammar check should always be done. Give the most polished, excellent product or presentation that you can. And make sure to do your work with integrity and a good attitude. Having a positive attitude and doing your job well is an excellent way to be a witness to the Lord at work. On the other hand, excessive complaining about your job or spending work hours on long personal phone calls is not only unprofessional, but shows a lack of work ethic that reflects on your individual character. Whatever you do, make sure you do it with excellence. That is how you can make your work truly beautiful, and be a witness to the Lord.

The Value of Vocation

And so, our work and what we do with our lives is important in many ways. Our work has the potential of lasting literally forever. We can make a mark in what we do in this life that will have value for eternity. As we work with excellence, we are a witness to the Lord. As we bridge friendships with nonbelievers we can win their souls to Christ. As we pray and faithfully serve the Lord day to day, we can experience His joy and blessing. To live a life focused on one's vocation is a wonderful thing. It is a celebration of God's divine purposes and calling.

REFLECT AND RESPOND

1.   Ask yourself the following questions:
   - What do you believe God is calling you to do?
   - What are some activities that you genuinely enjoy?
   - What experiences have made you happy?
   - What activities relax you?
   - What excites you about the future?

2.   How can you show kindness to someone where you work?

3.   What is something beautiful you can do through your work?

4.   Memorize Proverbs 31:30-31 "Charm is deceptive, and beauty is fleeting; but a woman who fears the LORD is to be praised. Give her the reward she has earned, and let her works bring her praise at the city gate.

Chapter Nine

RESTORER OF HOPE: The Gracious Woman in Service

"[She]... is well known for her good deeds, such as bringing up children, showing hospitality, washing the feet of the saints, helping those in trouble and devoting herself to all kinds of good deeds."
(I Timothy 5:10)

CALLED INTO SERVICE

We have spent the last two chapters looking at a woman's two main spheres of influence: her home and her work. Sometimes these two "worlds" seem all-consuming to a woman. Just ask any mother of preschoolers. She has to pencil in time just to take a shower! But as Christian women, we are called to look beyond our own families and jobs. We are called to look outward to serve God.

So often, we think we don't have the time or talents to serve God. We treat serving as something we will only consider when and if our schedules free us up to do so. We are sure that there are other people, other more talented and less busy people, who would be much better at serving anyway. Service is an option when it is convenient. Rick Warren, in his book *The Purpose Driven Life*, reminds us that service is at the heart of the Christian life.

> For Christians, service is not optional, something to be tacked onto our schedules if we can spare the time. It is the heart of the Christian life. Jesus came "to serve" and "to give" – and those two verbs should define your life on earth, too…. Jesus taught that spiritual maturity is never an end in itself. Maturity is for ministry! We grow up in order to give out. It is not enough to keep learning more and more. We must act on what we know and practice what we claim to believe.[48]

As gracious women, we are called to serve people in such a way that we restore their hope. You never know when one act of kindness will turn someone's heart from despair to trusting in God once again. Your presence and the Holy Spirit at work in you can be a powerful reminder that God still cares for them and that He is still actively involved in restoring wounded lives.

Women are uniquely created to be good at nurturing the wounded, caring for the sick, encouraging the weak. The woman described in Proverbs 31 was one that reached out to the needy in her community. Proverbs 31:20 tells us that "She opens her arms to the poor and extends her hands to the needy." I Timothy 5 gives a description of an older woman whose life has been rightly lived. Besides being faithful to her husband, she "is well known for her good deeds, such as bringing up children, showing hospitality, washing the feet of the saints, helping those in trouble and devoting herself to all kinds of good deeds." (I Timothy 5:10).

God has specially shaped you to be an altogether unique, one-of-a-kind expression of His love and compassion in the world. The spiritual gifts

He has given you, your life experiences and even your personality all work together to make you perfect for the service He calls you to. Some women think they must become someone else in order to serve. I often assumed that my naturally quiet, introverted nature needed to be transformed into a loud, outspoken personality in order to be useful to God, but I have learned that there are aspects of a quiet nature that God uses in order to reach other "quiet" people. God uses all sorts of personalities to reach all sorts of different people. So, recognize that God made you the way that you are and equipped you for the unique calling that He has for you.

God has called us to service. We are to serve Him and the purposes of His kingdom here on earth. Gracious women are those who order their lives to make serving God a priority, not just an afterthought. We are called to shine His light into the world around us. Gracious women are expressions of kindness in whatever capacity they are serving. And finally, we are called to present wounded hearts with God's magnificent offer of true beauty.

LET YOUR LIGHT SHINE

As women surrounded by family responsibilities, personal goals, grocery lists and unwashed laundry, it is sometimes too easy to become focused on our own lives and forget that there is a world at all beyond our own little worlds. We can even be consumed with very good things, like our own spiritual growth, caring for our families, and attending church. Those are all important things. But we can not get so focused on ourselves that we forget the world outside.

God continually calls us to look beyond ourselves and to the world outside of us. As we become more spiritually mature, we find that our focus becomes less and less on ourselves and more on God and those He loves. God calls us not only to bless us, but so that we can be a blessing to other people. It was the same for the nation of Israel. God chose Israel to be His special people. In Deuteronomy 7:6 God said, "For you are a people holy to the LORD your God. The LORD your God has chosen you out of all the peoples on the face of the earth to be his people, his treasured possession." But God did not choose Israel just so she could enjoy His blessings. Of course He wanted to bless her, but God chose her so that she could be a blessing to the nations around her. Isaiah 60:3 says, "Nations will come to your light, and kings to the brightness of your dawn." Israel was called to be a light pointing to the true God that all the peoples would recognize. And that is what we are called to be as well. God chose us and blessed us so that we could be a light shining into the world around us.

How can we serve the world around us? One of the very best ways that we can serve others is to be faithful in intercession. Intercession is praying to God on behalf of someone else. When you pray for a sick friend, you are interceding on their behalf. You are interceding for your neighbors when you pray for their salvation.

Prayer is truly an amazing thing. It takes only our time and willingness to let God teach and inspire us. Yet something as simple as prayer has the power to touch the world. All it takes is one faithful woman.

She can be a student, housewife, busy mother or career woman on the outside. On the inside, any woman can be a secret prayer warrior who is used by God to make a tremendous impact on the rest of the world. God has used hidden men and women throughout history to affect change in the lives of individuals and even in the outcome of nations through their persistent prayers. Rees Howells was a stellar example of a powerful intercessor who lived during the Welsh Revival. It is believed that his prayers were instrumental in the Battle of Britain, Dunkirk and D-Day. You will be amazed and inspired if you read the biographies and writings of prominent intercessors like David Brainerd, E.M. Bounds and Leonard Ravenhill. Each of them were faithful to pray and they touched countless lives on their knees.

So think about your own prayer life and how you can include intercession. Many times our prayers revolve around ourselves, our families, and perhaps a friend who has asked for prayer. But God wants us to pray with our eyes looking outward. Think of unsaved friends and relatives to pray for. Pray for your child's school teacher, your leaders at church and Christian mission organizations. Beyond that, God may give you a burden to pray for a specific people group or nation. Some people use a prayer calendar that lists unreached people groups. However you do it, include intercession as a regular part of your prayer life.

You may find that as you intercede for others, opportunities for serving them will somehow cross your path. Be open to the Holy Spirit leading you in specific ways to serve and bless other people. You may even find that the Lord will give you opportunities to bless strangers. Often times, we have a tendency to perceive other people as "machines" or just "background noise." When we go to a restaurant, our waiters are machines, built to serve us. Get one order wrong, and we sigh in disgust. When we go to the mall, the people around us function as background noise and part of the visual landscape. We kind of like it that they are there, but we don't care about them as human beings. But if you stop and really look at people with God's heart, you begin to notice the pain behind their eyes. Sometimes God will give you a word to say, or just a feeling to pray for them.

Jesus always saw people as people. John 1:35-42 gives an account of two disciples' first encounter with Jesus. Intrigued by Him, the two disciples asked him an unusual question, "Where are you staying?" Instead of brushing off their seemingly inconsequential question, Jesus invited them to stay with Him for the day so that they could see for themselves who He really was. I've always liked this story – to me, it shows how personal and accessible Jesus made Himself. Jesus didn't just see the demands of His ministry that lay ahead of Him, but that these two curious men were the ministry at hand!

Sometimes serving God happens as we go through life. If we open ourselves to God and allow ourselves to be accessible to people, we may find that the seeming "interruptions" that people make on our lives are divine opportunities to serve them. But other times we have to make service a priority to which we actively give ourselves. Giving can happen unexpectedly, but often we make plans to give. It is the same way with service. Sometimes you need to schedule ways to serve God and others into your life.

There are so many ways to serve if you are open to opportunities. Most churches are always looking for people who can serve in various capacities. Teaching Sunday school, caring for children in the nursery, greeting new visitors are all ways to serve within the church. Beyond the walls of your church, there are opportunities in your city. Volunteer opportunities abound not only in soup kitchens, crisis ministries and hospitals but in schools and neighborhood organizations. Most of them can take your time as you are able to give it. You just have to find an area of service and be faithful to making it a priority in your life.

NEVER UNDERESTIMATE KINDNESS

The funny thing about serving God is that it inevitably always takes the form of serving other people, whether it is people within His church or outside in the world. We can not serve God in a vacuum. In other words, we can't serve God without becoming involved with other human beings. God always calls us outward, to love people and to share His extravagant love for them through the simple power of kindness. We should never underestimate what a kind word or gesture can do.

Margaret Edson's Pulitzer award winning play, "Wit" tells the story of Dr. Vivian Bearing, an acclaimed, hard-nosed professor of the poet John Donne who is diagnosed with ovarian cancer and must face her own dying. Initially, she experiences the stages of her terminal illness through the lens of Donne's poetry and tries to intellectualize her suffering. But as she nears the end of her life, she gives up trying to make sense of what is happening to her. She finds little comfort in anything except the company of a nurse named Susie who brings her popsicle sticks and an old school teacher who reads her the children's classic *The Runaway Bunny*.

(With only minutes to live, Bearing gives up her championing of Donne:)

(*Quickly*) Now is not the time for verbal swordplay, for unlikely flights of imagination and wildly shifting perspectives, for metaphysical conceit, for wit.

And nothing could be worse than a detailed scholarly analysis. Erudition. Interpretation. Complication.

(*Slowly*) Now is a time for simplicity. Now is a time for, dare I say it, kindness.[49]

In the end it was a few simple acts of kindness that brought her comfort to ease the emotional pain of dying. The power of kindness is profoundly real.

It is interesting that when we see others in grief, we often respond by very simple gestures. We give flowers and bring food. Although these gestures can never mend the deep pains of suffering, what they do provide are powerful tokens of our connectedness. We offer a glimpse of beauty through flowers and the nourishment of physical sustenance through a home cooked meal. It is in such simple acts of kindness that God shows Himself to be present to those in need. Through our actions, God touches those who may be questioning whether He is really there at all.

When silence is seemingly deafening, our kindness can speak volumes.

Much of the sting of suffering, whether it is suffering caused by illness, loss, or other personal tragedy, is in the isolation that almost always accompanies suffering. People who are suffering often feel that no one understands what they are going through. They feel ashamed to tell anyone what has happened. When a kind soul comes alongside them and does nothing more that sit with them and listen carefully, it can mean the whole world to them. Having one faithful friend during suffering can be the difference between survival and despair. Margaret Mohrmann, in her book *Medicine as Ministry*, describes the power of a love in the face of suffering, in this case, in illness.

> Sickness is isolating; one of the pains that any serious illness inflicts is the pain of loneliness. The loneliness cannot be completely overcome, because sickness is, ultimately, an intensely personal experience. However, the loneliness that accompanies suffering, though it still may be present, can be stripped of much of its ability to destroy if it is transformed into a sign of the patient's unique and central position

within a community that focuses its healing love on him or her.[50]

Providing compassion and being present with those who are suffering, whether physically or emotionally, is an invaluable means of serving others. And it seems that women are often uniquely gifted for these vital ministries. Women are naturally nurturing. They provide physical touch and warmth easily. They readily enter into the sufferings of others. Women are often good counselors and able to listen to another person's troubles without jumping to judgment. As women, we should use our gifts to serve people and restore the hope they may have lost.

Kindness should be at the heart of all service and ministry. In fact, it is kindness that should motivate service, not skill or talent. I think sometimes we are scared off by the idea of Christian ministry because we think that ministry is only for those people who are well spoken and have degrees after their names. But to truly serve and to do ministry well is to do it with kindness, to care more concerned about other people than about showing our own worth.

Whether you serve God through teaching Sunday school, leading a Bible study, or organizing youth group, make sure you don't forget the heart of service. In all of your preparation and lesson plans, remember that true ministry is always about people, not presentations.

And make sure that you always make yourself available to being an instrument of kindness to another person, however insignificant they may appear to be. Sometimes high profile leaders can give off a whiff of superiority that makes "regular" people feel like they are unapproachable. People may be impressed by their teaching but feel threatened by them on a personal level. In contrast, Jesus, who was called a "Friend of Sinners," was always surrounded by people, by all sorts of people. He dined with them. He talked with them. I suspect the Pharisees probably watched in disbelief as Jesus conversed freely and laughed wholeheartedly around people. There was something about Him that made people feel like they would be welcomed, not rejected or spurned. He was approachable. He was all about kindness and people sensed it from the moment they saw Him.

There is a story called "The Cab Ride" in which a cab driver recounts a passenger he picked up over twenty years ago. She was an old woman in her 80s on her way to a hospice where she would spend the remaining weeks or months of her life. Instead of taking the shortest route to the hospice, the woman asked to take a scenic drive around the city. She told the driver where she lived as a young woman and the buildings she used to frequent. He listened patiently and actively. When they arrive at the hospice, several hours later, she asked the cab driver how much she owed him for the long ride, and the driver told her it would be free of charge.

> "You gave an old woman a little moment of joy," she said. "Thank you."

> I squeezed her hand, and then walked into the dim morning light. Behind me, a door shut. It was the sound of the closing of a life.

> I didn't pick up any more passengers that shift. I drove aimlessly lost in thought. For the rest of that day, I could hardly talk. What if that

woman had gotten an angry driver or one who was impatient to end his shift? What if I had refused to take the run, or had honked once, then driven away?

On a quick review, I don't think that I have done anything more important in my life. We're conditioned to think that our lives revolve around great moments. But great moments often catch us unaware - beautifully wrapped in what others may consider a small one.

People may not remember exactly what you did or what you said, but they will remember how you made them feel.[51]

We don't always realize how much we hurt others with a curt response or impatient brush off. We also don't recognize that how much a genuine smile or hug can do to show love to others. It is the little things we do and the small gestures of kindness that make all the difference in the world.

BEAUTY FOR ASHES

Isaiah 61:1-3 is a passage of Scripture that describes the Servant of the Lord. He has been anointed by the Holy Spirit to preach good news, heal the brokenhearted and release the captives. I am particularly captivated by verse 3 which depicts how God's Servant will provide for those who mourn in Zion. He will "bestow on them a crown of beauty instead of ashes, the oil of gladness instead of mourning, and a garment of praise instead of a spirit of despair." It is not only beautifully poetic, but is such a vivid picture of what God does for us. From the tops of our heads to the bottoms of our feet, He brings redemption to us. He gives life where there was death. He gives joy in the place of our tears.

In turn, this is the sort of ministry and service that we are called to. God calls us to participate with Him in the work of redemption, in bringing beauty for ashes, joy for sorrow, and praise for despair. Think about a beautiful crown studded with the finest jewels. Crowns mark royalty, signify champions and bring honor to whoever wears them. Then contrast that with an image of ashes. Ashes are a symbol of death. They are the only remains of life when it passes through fire, and were used in mourning. They are the difference between night and day. When God redeems a life, it is so drastically changed that it is like night and day.

The truth is that when God redeems us, our inner transformation is often accompanied by external changes as well. We reflect on the outside what is going on inside. When we are physically sick, the last thing on our mind is our physical appearance. When we are grieving on the inside, people can almost always tell just by looking at us. But when we are excited about something, we can't keep from smiling. When we are happy, our faces and body language show it on the outside.

During my sophomore year of college, I lived down the hall from a girl named Caitlyn who had been clinically diagnosed with schizophrenia. She was used to tell me that she saw demons in her dorm room. I visited her room on occasion, and it was always dimly lit. Unlike most other dorm rooms, there were no posters on the wall, no pretty things decorating her desk. From the bare cinderblock walls to the plain hard floors, the room itself felt depressed. Caitlyn's room was an outward expression of what was going on inside of her. I sometimes imagined her room transformed. I pictured it full of beautiful things, blooming flowers and pretty keepsakes… outward things that symbolized the beautiful changes occurring in her soul.

God wants to do that for us and for those whom we touch. From the very core of our souls to the outward expression of our lives, He wants our lives to be full of beauty. I love the saying, "A heart full of love produces a life full of beauty." Beauty is an expression of the fullness of love from our hearts. As we are filled with God's incredible love, our lives become works of art, expressions of abundance and beauty. As you serve God through serving people, their lives in turn will be touched by beauty.

A SERVANT'S REWARD

As we come to the end of our treatise on gracious living, it isn't a coincidence that we conclude with service. We end with service not because serving is less important than our home or work life. Nor is it an afterthought. On the contrary, as we grow in

Christian maturity and in becoming gracious women, the natural result is that we begin to look outward, towards other people, particularly those outside of our families and circle of friends. Graciousness is always an outreaching expression of God's grace towards others. As we become more gracious, we find that we begin to focus less on ourselves and more on others. We begin to serve people in our words and actions. We become an expression of God's grace to the world.

GRACIOUS LIVING FOR A LIFETIME

Becoming a gracious woman is a lifelong journey and an everyday exercise. By God's grace, you can become the truly gracious woman that He has called you to be, inside and out. You can live out the principles of order, kindness and beauty in all of your relationships: as a wife, mother and friend. You can also practice gracious living through your home, job and acts of service. I don't think any of us will ever become the perfect woman, but part of being a gracious woman is accepting the process of growth in our own lives. We will make mistakes and sometimes fail miserably along the way, but by God's grace, He will form His gracious image in us. We can be the gracious women He has called us to be!

REFLECT AND RESPOND

1. How can you make serving God and others a priority in your life?

2. What are some ways you can express kindness through serving people? How are some ways people inadvertently make others feel badly?

3. Read Isaiah 61:1-3. This passage describes the Servant of the Lord. What is He called to do?

4. Memorize I Timothy 5:10 "[She]…is well known for her good deeds, such as bringing up children, showing hospitality, washing the feet of the saints, helping those in trouble and devoting herself to all kinds of good deeds."

REFERENCES

Chapter One

[1] Alec Waugh, modified slightly.

[2] Emilie Barnes, *The Spirit of Loveliness* (Eugene: Harvest House Publishers, 1992), 43-44.

Chapter Two

[3] Matthew 6:9-13.

[4] Andrew Murray, *Humility: The Journey Toward Holiness* (Minneapolis: Bethany House Publishers, 2001).

[5] A.W. Tozer, *The Pursuit of God: The Human Thirst for the Divine* (Camp Hill: Christian Publications, 1993), 13.

Chapter Three

[6] Sam Levenson, "Time Tested Beauty Tips." This poem is often attributed to Audrey Hepburn, but was in fact written by Sam Levenson. Hepburn loved the poem and read it to her children.

[7] Alexandra Stoddard, *Living a Beautiful Life* (New York: Avon Books, 1986), 43.

[8] Ingrid Trobisch, *The Confident Woman* (New York: Harper Collins, 1993), 20.

[9] Enid Haupt, modified slightly.

[10] Joyce Landort, *The Fragrance of Beauty: Practical Ways to Charm Focusing on the Inner You* (Wheaton: Victor Books, 1975), 103.

[11] Todd Kappelman, "A Return to Modesty", Probe Ministries, 2001.

[12] Landort, 103.

[13] Spina, Robert, "Rose: Portrait of a Woman," The Golden Girls, Original Air Date: 1992.

Chapter Four

[14] Mike Mason, *The Mystery of Marriage* (Sisters: Multnomah Press, 1985), 58-59.

[15] Ephesians 5:25-33.

[16] Walter Wangerin, Jr., "Forgiveness: The Divine Absurdity," *The Making of a Marriage* (Nashville: Thomas Nelson Publishers, 1993), 108.

[17] Gary Smalley, *For Better or For Best: Understand Your Man* (Grand Rapids: Zondervan Publishing, 1979) 83.

[18] Proverbs 21:9, 25:24.

[19] Daisy Eyebright, "A Manual of Etiquette with Hints on Politeness and Good Breeding" (1884). This Victorian guide included a section on advice directed to wives. A few points are illustrated below.

> A pleasant, cheerful wife is as a rainbow, set in the sky, when her husband's mind is beset with storms and tempests; but a dissatisfied and fretful wife, in the hour of trouble, is like one of those fiends who are appointed to torture the lost spirits."

> And don't think that when you have obtained a husband your attention to personal neatness, and deportment should be relaxed. Now, in truth, is the important time for you to exhibit superior taste, and excellence in the cultivation of your address, and the becoming elegance of your appearance.

> If it required some care to retain the admiration of your lover, be sure that much more is desired to keep yourself lovely in the eyes of your husband.

> Don't prove the truth of the trite proverb that *"Familiarity breeds contempt."* If it were due to your lover to always maintain a neat and ladylike aspect, how much more is he entitled to a similar mark of respect who has linked all his hopes of future happiness with yours?

> And if you can manage these matters without the appearance of studying them, so much the more

attractive will you become.

For there are husbands who grow impatient of the daily routine of the toilette, especially, if the wife is very slow and dilatory about it; and it is better to be ready dressed to meet them, when they return to dinner or supper, and all prepared to give them a smiling and cordial welcome. A husband dislikes to return to his home after a hard day's work, and find his wife *en dishabille,* and the house in confusion.

So make yourself sweet, and lovely; and your surroundings the same; and let him find the household ready to receive him; and dinner or supper promptly, and toothsomely prepared.

A sweet temper carries its password in the face -- a sweet and cheerful countenance; and such a disposition is like a jar of honey, which turns all that drops into it to candied sugar, and honeyed sweetness.

Women are a blessing to every circle in which they move, if they will but cultivate a cheerful, happy, blithesome disposition.

Domestic troubles will arise, and domestic storms may sweep over the home, but the cheerful wife will possess the power to rise above them all; and a quiet, meek, submissive spirit, will bring her to a safe harbor.

A good temper *can be* cultivated, although it is a hard task to do so; yet a strong will *can* curb the fiery passion which surges through the heart; and can keep in hand the prancing, racing, leaping coursers of anger and fury.

There are wives, doubtless, who possess peppered tempers, spiced with cayenne; are fiery furnaces, and when fuel is given to them they wax hotter and hotter, until the fire scorches, and burns with fury. But there are no more fiery-tempered wives than there are husbands, and a good-tempered husband can control a fiery-tempered wife with ease. Being let alone, left to oneself until the fire is reduced to ashy paleness, is the best remedy for this disease, when it shows itself in either sex. A good wife, however, is wisdom, courage, strength, and endurance to a man; while a bad one is confusion, discomfiture, weakness, and *despair.*

"Oh, what a treasure is a virtuous wife,
Discreet and loving! Not one gift on earth
Makes a man's life so nighly bound to Heaven.
She gives him double forces to endure,
And to enjoy, by being one with him,
Feeling his joys and griefs with equal sense.
Gold is right precious, but its price affects
With pride and avarice.
But a true wife both sense and soul delights,
And mixeth not her good with any ill.
Her virtues, ruling hearts, all powers command;
All store without her leaves a man but poor,
And with her, poverty is exceeding store;
No time is tedious with her, her true worth
Makes a true husband think his arms enfold,
(With her alone,) a complete world of gold."

[20] Elisabeth Elliot, *Let Me Be a Woman* (Wheaton: Tyndale House Publishers, 1976), 105-106.
[21] Ingrid Trobisch, *The Confident Woman* (New York: Harper Collins, 1993), 69.
[22] Ibid, 118.

Chapter Five
[23] In 2003, Barbara Kisilevsky, PhD, of Queens University in Ontario, Canada conducted a study on 60 fetuses between 38-40 weeks gestation in Hangzhou, China. Half of the fetuses

were played a 2-minute recording of a poem read by their mothers while the other half heard a recording read by a stranger. When the fetuses who heard the recording of their mother's voices, their heart rate increased throughout the entire recording and remained high for two minutes after the recording ended. The fetuses who heard the recording by a stranger showed decreased heart rates.

Chapter Six

[24] Trobisch, 63.

[25] L.M. Montgomery, Anne of Green Gables (New York: Grosset and Dunlap, 1908), 222.

[26] Landort, 100.

[27] Margaret Guenther, *Holy Listening: The Art of Spiritual Direction* (Cowley Publications, 1992).

[28] David G. Benner, *Care of Souls: Revisioning Christian Nurture and Counsel* (Baker Book House, 1998), 153.

[29] Stoddard, 152.

Chapter Seven

[30] Victoria Magazine, *Intimate Home: Creating a Private World* (New York: Hearst Books, 1992), 8-9.

[31] J.R. Miller, D.D., *Secrets of Happy Home Life: What Have You to Do With It?*, 1894.

[32] Stoddard, 18.

[33] Victoria Magazine, 10.

[34] Stoddard, 3.

[35] Edith Schaeffer, *The Hidden Art of Homemaking* (Wheaton: Tyndale House Publishers, 1971), 124

[36] Ravi Zacharias, Jesus Among Other Gods (Nashville: Word Publishing, 2000), 44-45.

[37] Dorothy C. Bass, *Receiving the Day: Christian Practices for Opening the Gift of Time*, John Wiley & Sons, 2001.

[38] Proverbs 15:17, 17:1.

[39] Schaeffer, 104-105.

[40] Ibid., 120.

[41] Stoddard, 70.

[42] "A Mother's Touch," *Victoria Magazine,* May 1998.

Chapter Eight

[43] Frederick Buechner, *Listening to Your Life* (San Francisco: Harper Collins, 1992), 185-186.

[44] Philip Yancey, *Reaching for the Invisible God: What Can We Expect to Find?* (Grand Rapids: Zondervan Publishing House, 2000), 221.

[45] Rick Warren, *The Purpose Driven Life* (Grand Rapids: Zondervan Publishing, 2002), 32-33.

[46] Margaret E. Mohrmann, MD *Medicine as Ministry* (Cleveland: Pilgrim Press, 1995), 49.

[47] Eugene H. Peterson, *A Long Obedience in the Same Direction* (Downers Grove: InterVarsity Press, 1980), 106-107.

Chapter Nine

[48] Warren, 230-231.

[49] Margaret Edson, *Wit* (New York: Faber and Faber, 1999).

[50] Mohrmann, 85-86.

[51] "The Cab Ride," Anonymous.

www.ingramcontent.com/pod-product-compliance
Lightning Source LLC
LaVergne TN
LVHW041213080426
835508LV00011B/941